THY NAME IS LIFE

SUJOY ROY

BLUEROSE PUBLISHERS
India | U.K.

Copyright © Sujoy Roy 2024

All rights reserved by author. No part of this publication may be reproduced, stored in a retrieval system or transmitted in any form or by any means, electronic, mechanical, photocopying, recording or otherwise, without the prior permission of the author. Although every precaution has been taken to verify the accuracy of the information contained herein, the publisher assumes no responsibility for any errors or omissions. No liability is assumed for damages that may result from the use of information contained within.

BlueRose Publishers takes no responsibility for any damages, losses, or liabilities that may arise from the use or misuse of the information, products, or services provided in this publication.

For permissions requests or inquiries regarding this publication, please contact:

BLUEROSE PUBLISHERS
www.BlueRoseONE.com
info@bluerosepublishers.com
+91 8882 898 898
+4407342408967

ISBN: 978-93-5989-753-0

Cover design: Muskan Sacheva
Typesetting: Rohit

First Edition: February 2024

Dedication

This book is dedicated to all those warriors who are battling against the deadly enemy: Cancer and those who have succumbed to it after a prolonged battle. This is to honor their battles.

•••

Dear Diary, I have not spoken to you for a long time. There is nothing much to say or write, though. All my thoughts are just fading away into oblivion. No one cares; no one bothers what people think or feel. People do not have time to ponder over trivial things. They already have so much on their plates that things like love, friendship, and relationships don't matter to them anymore. They have bigger things to engage themselves in, utilize their time on, and achieve in life. Many of the things that I am writing shouldn't matter to anyone because people have less time and more work. In pursuit of higher ambitions, people forget each other, let alone this small piece of paper.

Probably in the next few days, even I will forget that I have spoken to you. Maybe I wouldn't speak to you for a few months together. Just like my thoughts, you would also fade away in my memory. But I know you will remember me. You do not forget anyone. You preserve the most important memories of everyone's life, whether they are good, bad, or ugly.

So I entrust it to you to preserve mine as well.

•••

TRANSLATOR'S PREFACE

•••

This is the story of Badshah, a young, vibrant, lively young man who succumbed to GBM, or Glioblastoma, on 13 February 2017. He was all of twenty-eight years old. For eight months he fought this dreaded disease, with the full support of his family and friends. But the battle ended on a departing note. Is the tragic note the dominant note in this narrative? Rather, is that the only way to perceive a tragedy? Is triumph only to be measured as acontradiction to ending? Badshah, or Avik, had lived life larger than king size. His enthusiasm for football, hiscompassionate and amicable nature, his efficiency and skill at his place of work, had won him friends, admirers, accolades and empathy by the buckets. If one were to see it all in one frame, it would far outweigh a life of twenty-eight years.This narrative is penned by Avik's father, Sujoy Roy. It is fictionalized only to the point of changing some of the names. Otherwise, the epic saga of Badshah's life, in the living and the dying, has been recorded and reconstructed faithfully by his loving father. In celebrating a life, a positive attitude, a philosophical outlook, an ambitious vision, some dreams and hopes and an energetically throbbing heart, this narrative has successfully immortalized the lively young man called Badshah. When I received the original published volume in Bengali, I finished reading it in the span of a few quick hours. The volume came with a request for me to translate it into English. Having recently undergone a similar struggle with a different kind of cancer, I had barely emerged alive but my soul was reeling from the storm of stress and emotional upheaval that this disease usually brings for the patient and the family. It was an instant bond that was forged between Badshah and me, as I identified with almost everything that he and his family endured while treating the disease. But over and above all else, the positivity of the family, the extreme fortitude of the near and dear ones and Badshah's lingering smile touched me personally as a reader. Breaking through the fourth dimension, Avik seemed to soar to the level of Death and stand as an equal, celebrating life through the quality of living and not measuring it in units of time such as years, months and days.I felt it would be a privilege and an honour to translate this epic tome into English. But unfortunately, midway through the journey, I had to seek help due to health issues of my own. Samrat Maitra, the co-translator of this book, came to my rescue at this point and together we were able to complete the task. In parting, I wish this book, its author and its protagonist all the very best as they sail through every reader's mindscape and live life. afresh. May Badshah be reborn in each reading of this published volume!

Sreejata Guha

Co-translator with Samrat Maitra.

ABOUT THE AUTHOR

•••

Mr. Sujoy Roy, the eldest son of Sudhendu and Manju Roy, was born on July 16, 1952. He received his primary education from Jagabandhu Institution, Kolkata. On January 1, 1964, his family shifted their base from Kolkata to Patna in search of better business opportunities. From the age of 11, he was enrolled at Raja Ram Mohan Roy Seminary. He graduated from Patna University in 1975. During the political turmoil of 1974 (the movement led by the late Mr. Jaiprakash Narayan), he had to take a break for a year to participate in the movement. Later, he was greatly influenced by Marxism. To stabilize his family, Roy had to join the Bank of Baroda in 1978. He was also involved in the trade union activities of the bank. Roy got married to Shyamali Roy in 1983. In 1992, he was transferred to Jamshedpur, from where he later retired in 2012.

Since his adolescence, Roy sought solace in writing. He penned his novel, in Bengali, 'Glioblastoma O Ekti Akhyan' after the demise of his son. Prior to that, he had published an anthology of poems and his second novel, in Bengali, 'Britto Bhenge'. Apart from this, many of his short stories have been published in noted Bengali weeklies. Roy has also written various articles for different dailies.

ABOUT THE TRANSLATORS

Sreejata Guha is a student of literature by discipline, with an MA in Comparative Literature from SUNY at Stony Brook, USA. She has to her name over a dozen translated titles, published in India by Penguin Books India Pvt. Limited and Hachette India. A reader, a catalyst, and a raconteur (in that order), she is passionate about bridging gaps and communication. This manuscript came into her hands as a commissioned project, and she was deeply impressed by the quality of writing and the depth of emotion contained within these pages, which made her take it on.

Samrat Maitra, a village school master, is passionate about reading, writing, sports, and trivia. He has penned short stories, articles, and quiz columns for several distinguished periodicals and magazines. An enthusiastic translator, he has also co-authored 'Bish Bishom', a pastiche on the lesser mortals of Bengali literature.

CONTENTS

•••

TRANSLATOR'S PREFACE	vi
ABOUT THE AUTHOR	ix
ABOUT THE TRANSLATORS	xi
SEIZURE	1
BAD NEWS	15
15 JULY	32
COLUMBIA ASIA	38
SURGERY	52
DEADLY DISEASE	64
ON THE WAY TO MUMBAI	76
NEW CITY	91
THE AWAKENING OF A NEW CONSCIOUSNESS	113
TURBULENT TIMES	127
LURED BY LIVELIHOOD	136
TMH	155
IN HIS CITY	174
NANAWATI	180
KOKILABEN	200

NEW YEAR	220
SHUNTING	235
CABIN 12	245
CCU	253
VENTILATION	263
ARSENAL	273
ACKNOWLEDGMENT	278
SYNOPSIS	280

1

SEIZURE

...

It happened exactly at the moment that the cab reached Ranchi Airport, after taking a complete U-turn. Badshah's body seemed to grow stiff. His eyes rolled up. The instant that Sanjay opened the car door, Badshah got off. Sitting next to him, Mili tried to stop him, but she couldn't. If Sanjay had not reached out with both arms and held him fast, Badshah would have fallen flat on his face. In this situation, it was quite natural that Sanjay screamed for help. A few people came forward at his mercy to: a few co-passengers, a few who had come to see them off, and some security personnel as well. Authorities were summoned from within the airport, a wheelchair was arranged and Badshah was made to sit in it. Nearly seven or eight seconds later the symptoms of the fit receded. Later, in Mumbai, Sanjay came to know that such fits were called 'seizures' in medical terminology.

Once Badshah grew calmer, he was wheeled into the airport and made to sit on a reasonably comfortable seat. Mili gave him some glucose solution and a paracetamol. She had carried these from their home in Jamshedpur, on the advice of the doctor. He had said this would alleviate the headaches. It did, albeit temporarily. But the doctor hadn't foreseen a seizure, or even if he had, didn't mention it. Neither Sanjay nor Mili had an inkling that this could happen. And they did not know how to handle a seizure.

When Badshah seemed a little better, Sanjay proceeded to check their luggage in. It was all of two suitcases—one for Sanjay and Mili and the other one for Badshah. One entire suitcase was needed to carry all his clothes, shoes, medicines, medical files, etc. Although they did not know for how long they were going to Mumbai, Mili wanted to dress up her son in bright and fresh clothes. She did not want him to look dull just because he was unwell.

After checking the luggage in, Sanjay began to scout for medical assistance at the airport. Mili sat by Badshah all through. Badshah rested his head on his mother's lap peacefully. It was impossible to believe that a few minutes ago he had undergone a seizure.

Eventually, a doctor was located. He was seated in a mid-sized room in the Arrival Lounge, along with a female assistant. When Sanjay narrated the events to him, he and his assistant immediately went to take a look at Badshah. He examined Badshah's eyes for dilation, checked his pulse and blood pressure, and then spoke to Sanjay at length collecting all the details of the case. Finally, he said, 'There isn't much that I can do. But instead of giving him glucose solution, please give him Electral. And in case of headaches, do give him paracetamol.'

Thereafter the doctor spoke to the Indigo Airlines authorities to ensure that Badshah got a smooth passage into the aircraft at the time of boarding. Meanwhile, the assistant doctor organized the 'Electral' for him. The glucose solution was discarded. Both Mili and Sanjay were gratified at this kind of concern and care demonstrated by the medical personnel. And Badshah's pained face too bore the traces of relief—it was good to know that even in this airport there is help at hand! Since the day that the twenty-eight-year-old, bright, energetic boy had come to know that there was a tumour in his brain and that it was cancerous, he had begun to shatter into bits deep inside. He would still talk to his friends and family with his usual amicability because that was second nature to him. But his secret tears would often come to light, in his melancholic gaze, his pained glances. Sanjay or Mili did not know whether Badshah was aware that he was suffering from Glioblastoma or GBM. It was the most aggressive and the most critical of brain tumours—because it keeps recurring. Glioblastoma was almost a death sentence—that is what Sanjay and Mili had heard people say, but they hadn't cared to find out for themselves. Nowadays a Google search would present every little detail to you. As a matter of fact, they did not have the urge or the courage to find out for themselves. Much later, Mili had culled this fact out of the internet and shared it with Sanjay—perhaps as a means to console their grieving hearts.

Be that as it may. Meanwhile, there had been a very unfortunate announcement: the flight was late by four hours. Just before leaving Jamshedpur Sanjay had received a message update from Indigo Airlines. That was a delay of an hour. On their way to Ranchi there was another message, making it two hours. But now the announcement was terrifying—fo—ur full hours late. So the flight that was to have departed at a quarter past four would now leave at a quarter past eight. With Badshah in this condition, Sanjay felt his mouth go dry with fear. Mili's state was no better, as was evident from her face. Badshah was updated of on the new turn of events. He sat on the sofa with his eyes shut tight.

Sanjay felt the ground had vanished from beneath his feet. In this condition, he just prayed they would allow him to fly. God knew how long he would be stable. If his condition worsened, if there was another seizure, they wouldn't let him to board the flight. What would Sanjay do then? Should they go back to Jamshedpur with Bandshah or should they battle it out for four hours and try to board the flight to Mumbai? He held in his hand a Fit-to-Fly certificate endorsed by Dr. Das of the colony. He was aware of Badshah's case. He had been monitoring Badshah and although he didn't know the reason for the headaches and nausea, he had prescribed an MRI and advised them on where to do it. But that Fit-to-Fly certificate was of no use now, especially after the seizure. The airport doctor had been most helpful. So perhaps it would be possible to board the flight with the help of the authorities. He just hoped there were no more seizures.

Sanjay could not even discuss this with Mili because Badshah was resting his head on his mother's lap and trying to sleep. Trying to, but not succeeding since Ranchi airport had no long sofas where he could be made to lie down. There were only comfortable chairs with armrests, which were good for seating, but not lying down. Badshah sat on one chair and leaned over to rest his head on his mother's lap, who sat in the next chair. Despite battling cancer for the past eight months, despite tolerating the torturous journey of radiation and chemotherapy, Badshah's face did not bear the gloom of melancholy. His face was vibrant and alive, with all the hope and fervor to live, to survive. In the past few months of a long, unending tunnel of illness, whenever Badshah had met someone, whenever he had gone somewhere, his face had glowed with the light of this zeal to live. Perhaps that is why he was loved wherever he went.

Sanjay stole a glance at Badshah's face, resting on Mili's lap—a unique glow of bliss, an aura of a life lived fully. Suddenly Sanjay started as he realized the time: it was a quarter past five. So, another three full hours to go. Each moment felt like a full year. Sanjay stopped trying to keep track of the time—of when a quarter past eight would arrive. He sat down in the chair next to Mili, feeling exhausted. As he dozed, Badshah sipped on the Electral solution that Mili offered him every few minutes.

At this moment Sanjay's mobile phone rang. It was Rintu from Mumbai. That was Sanjay's younger brother. He was fully updated on every detail of Badshah's illness and treatment and as involved as Sanjay and Mili.

2 May 2016, the day that Badshah had undergone an MRI in Bangalore's Columbia Asia Hospital, and his brain tumour was first diagnosed, was also the date from which Rintu had been fully involved with each detail, sometimes perhaps even more than Mili and Sanjay. The entire treatment in Mumbai had been conducted from Rintu's home. Nearly two and a half months, he had gone with Badshah to Tata Memorial Hospital for the radiation and chemotherapy. From getting a hold of the doctors for a discussion, to standing in long queues to buy medicines, Rintu had taken a lot upon himself. Sanjay and Mili gained a lot of relief, thanks to his efforts. Naturally, it was very hard for parents to stay calm and steady when their son was afflicted with brain cancer at such a young age, and that too GBM—which was akin to a death sentence. Rintu was very aware of that.

Rintu had started calling even before they left Jamshedpur for Ranchi. Sanjay was updating him on every little detail, just as Rintu was aware of the few days just before that—Badshah's headaches, vomiting, the doctor in Jamshedpur, and the rushed decision to take him to Mumbai again. This time he must be calling for the latest update on Badshah's condition.

Sanjay took the call, 'Hello, yes, they have just announced that the flight is late by four hours.' 'Four hours!' Rintu sounded very worried. 'Yes, four hours,' Sanjay confirmed. So, if it departed at a quarter past eight, they would reach Mumbai close to eleven in the night. Rintu asked, 'How is Badshah?' 'Resting, but not comfortably. There are no sofas here where he can stretch out.' At this Rintu suggested, 'Why don't you check if they have a resting room somewhere in the airport. If there is one, check into it and make him lie down. There's still a very long time to go.'

Sanjay began to look for a sick room or a resting room. The authorities at Indigo airlines said that these rooms are in the control of the Airports Authority of India. Worrying about Badshah's comfort and the need to give him a proper bed to rest on, Sanjay rushed to get a hold of the AAI authorities. He was informed that none of the rooms were available. There were five rooms in all, and they had been booked in advance, as per the rules. These rooms were all on the first floor. Sanjay too the lift and went upstairs to check the rooms which were right above the Arrival zone. Three rooms were locked and bolted from the outside, no one could tell who had taken those rooms. The other two rooms were occupied. He saw a couple of young children playing outside the rooms and he could hear female voices inside. Sanjay tried to speak to them, but to no avail. So, he began to look for other possibilities. Near the resting rooms, there was an empty corridor of the same length. He checked it out as a possible spot where something could be spread out and Badshah could be made to lie down. He came downstairs and after speaking with Mili, decided to take Badshah to that spot he had checked out. A wheelchair was already at their disposal for Badshah. They took the lift and brought him up to the first floor. In that corridor space, Mili spread out her shawl on the floor. It was a cold evening at the end of December, and that too the winter of Ranchi, which was always a trifle colder than even Jamshedpur. The airport was outside the city and hence a few degrees cooler. Badshah sat down on the shawl, touched the floor w,ith his left hand and refused to lie on the floor, despite the shawl spread upon it. It was only his left hand and leg that were functional. Ever since the surgery on 5 May 2016, Badshah's right arm and leg were not functional. Even after almost six months of physiotherapy, now in December, his right side was still far from being normal again. Therefore, his left hand was as good as his right hand. He tested the floor with his left hand and stood up, only to seat himself in the wheelchair again.

Sanjay and Mili were at their wits' end. There were still a few hours to go before boarding the flight. How would these hours pass, how would Badshah sit in the wheelchair for all this time? Sanjay and Mili glanced at each other and then their gaze rested on Badshah—a piercing pain shot through their beings. They had not wanted to accept that this disease was incurable. They had heard people whisper, people who had looked up the internet; but they were not ready to accept it, neither had they wanted to know more. Which parent would wish to know more about their child's illness? Besides, miracles did happen. Medical miracles. Why, just the other day someone said they'd seen on TV, a GBM patient had recovered fully and was playing football, and riding bikes! Sanjay wondered—couldn't such a miracle happen to his son, Badshah?

Suddenly he came back to the present. Badshah was sitting in the wheelchair, his eyes shut and his arms folded across his heart. Have they ever felt more vulnerable? Sanjay and Mili were standing beside Badshah, their fingers gently caressing him, so that he did not feel they were far from him. They exchanged a glance full of pain and helplessness. If only they could do something to set Badshah at ease, to give him the comfort of stretching out on a bed, or even a sofa.

All of a sudden, they could hear a door being unlocked. A young man stood in front of the resting room number three, trying to unlock the bolt. He was about thirtyyearsold or thereabouts, of a slight build and a pleasant disposition. As soon as he unlocked the door and stepped into the room, Sanjay rushed towards the room. He conveyed their situation and pleaded for assistance—to let Badshah lie down on one of the beds. Sanjay had noticed that there were two beds in the room. At first, there was some hesitation, but when he saw Badshah, he agreed. Sanjay had tears in his eyes, as he fetched Badshah on his wheelchair and somehow managed to get him onto the bed. Badshah was completely drained and exhausted by then. But he looked visibly at ease as he lay down on the bed. One glance to see where his mother was, and he was even more at peace as he drifted off to sleep.

Sanjay began to converse with their benefactor. He was from a small town in Odisha. His name was Prabhat Mohanty. He had worked at Bhubaneshwar Airport for a few years and had been recently transferred to Ranchi. He was entitled to living quarters, as an employee of AAI, but since one wasn't allocated to him yet, he had been given one of the resting rooms instead. He was an affable man and he asked about Badshah's condition in detail. On knowing the whole story, he grew sad. Then he mused that a lot of youngsters were getting afflicted with brain cancer these days and he wondered if the root of it had anything to do with the excessive use of technology such as computers, cell phones, etc. Sanjay had no answer to this question, but he too felt that it was high time some attention and some thought was devoted to this subject.

Badshah was fast asleep. Mili was half-lying beside him and resting. It was nearly six-thirty. Sanjay felt like some tea. Both Mr. Mohanty and Mili declined. So, he walked up to the airport restaurant that was very near the resting rooms, and asked for a cup of tea.

Over tea he updated Rintu, who was greatly relieved to know that Badshah had found a place to lie down and was sleeping peacefully. Rintu also suggested that since it would be nearly eleven-thirty when they would come out of Mumbai airport, perhaps they should take Badshah directly to the hospital. The treatment would also begin straightaway. Sanjay liked the idea. Immediate medical attention for Badshah was tempting indeed, instead of wasting a night at home.

When he returned to the room, he mentioned it to Mili. She agreed, 'Rintu is absolutely right.' They looked at Badshah. He was still fast asleep. Sanjay had picked up a packet of biscuits. He handed it to Mili, 'Here, you haven't eaten anything in a long while.' Mili opened the packet and handed two biscuits to Sanjay. Suddenly he realized that he was quite hungry. He wondered if tension increased hunger or the other way around. Did hunger make itself felt once the period of stress had ended? *Had* it ended for them—was Badshah fine now? Not exactly. But at least he was stable now. There had been no further seizures. He was sleeping peacefully. Sanjay sat down on a chair.

Mili too was looking calmer. She had squeezed in beside Badshah and stretched out on the bed. Sanjay checked his watch. There was still an hour to go. Prabhat was resting on the other bed. Suddenly there was an uproar in the distance. Sanjay stepped into the corridor and peered over the railing. Two passengers were engaged in a loud dispute with the staff of Indigo Airlines. The passengers were more aggressive and the Airline staff looked defensive. The subject of the dispute remained unclear, but within ten minutes it seemed to be resolved. Sanjay went downstairs and took a round of the security zone in the hope of gaining some familiarity with the security personnel. After all, in a short while, Badshah would have to take on this hurdle. The problem was that after his seizure, the doctor's certificate that they had procured in Jamshedpur seemed to be invalid. The airline's staff were reluctant to accept it at face value. Thankfully, the airport doctor did not pen down anything equally negative or hostile in his report. Sanjay had already tried to speak to the authorities once. They had consented to let him board the flight. Sanjay went in search of the Manager, in the hope of reconfirming that assurance.

He was a good man who seemed to understand the urgency of Badshah reaching Mumbai. All he asked was, 'There will not be an issue with the oxygen levels after takeoff, will there?' Sanjay had immediately reassured him that there was no such danger. Then he asked, 'Is your son all right now?' When Sanjay replied in the affirmative, the man said, 'Go on and take him to Mumbai. There is no treatment for this disease in these parts. At least in Mumbai they will be able to treat him.' Sanjay heaved a sigh of relief. It was getting closer to the departure time now. He went back to the resting room to start getting Badshah ready.

Badshah was still lying with his eyes shut. It was hard to tell whether he was sleeping or just exhausted beyond words. Mili informed him that Badshah had woken up, but he was reluctant to sit up on the bed. Sanjay said, 'That's all right. Let him lie down for a little longer.'

About half an hour later came the announcement that the Indogo Airlines Mumbai-Patna-Ranchi flight had just landed. After twnty minutes or so, passengers to Mumbai should head towards security check.

It was time to get Badshah going. Mili called him softly, 'Badu, Badu, we have to go now, son. Wake up.' Badshah glanced at Mili gently and said, 'I will.' By then, Sanjay had summoned the wheelchair pusher. After his shoes were slid onto his feet, Badshah was seated on the wheelchair. The pusher began to wheel him towards the lift as Mili and Sanjay bade Prabhat goodbye. Sanjay conveyed his heartfelt gratitude to him one more time. Prabhat responded by saying that he too ha enjoyed being of use, and he wished Badshah a speedy recovery.

Before entering the security zone, Sanjay coached Badshah for any questions and how to answer it. The security staff asked why he was in a wheelchair and what was he suffering from. Badshah replied, 'Brain tumour.' He also mentioned that post-surgery his hands and legs were weak and hence the wheelchair. The hair on Badshah's head was not uniform: it was patchy and thin. It was obviously an effect of chemotherapy. Many people could guess from his hair that he was a cancer patient. The security staff did not ask any other questions.

Once they entered the boarding lounge, Sanjay asked Badshah, 'Do you want to eat something?' Badshah asked, 'Do you have any biscuits?' Mili had some in her bag. She handed him a few. Sanjay asked again, 'Do you want tea?' When Badshah nodded, Sanjay went up to the airport counter and got two cups of tea, for Badshah and himself. Mili did not really like too many cups of tea in a day.

As soon as they finished their tea, the boarding announcement started. The wheelchair pusher began to move ahead with Badshah, closely followed by Sanjay and Mili. They had reserved seats in the first row of the aircraft.

Sanjay had booked these seats at a premium price because anything else would have been uncomfortable for Badshah. It would be hard for him to walk to those, and the wheelchair wouldn't go so far in—the toilet too would be a challenge.

Badshah was very relieved to get the first-row seats. Mili made him sit be the window and she took the middle seat. When all the passengers had boarded, the aircraft started preparing to fly. Sanjay checked his watch. It was exactly a quarter past eight. The journey to Mumbai took two hours and fifteen minutes. So, they would land in Mumbai at ten thirty. Sanjay was comforted by the thought of Rintu was waiting outside the airport with the ambulance. With the worries and the stress, Sanjay too felt a bit enervated. As the flight gained speed before takeoff, his body felt light. Sanjay leaned back in his seat and his eyes drifted shut.

BAD NEWS

•••

2 May 2016. Sanjay and a few others were sitting in the Building Society office. It was ten minutes past nine in the night. Suddenly Sanjay received a call on his mobile phone. It was an unknown number. The voice at the other end said, 'Uncle, I am Avik's friend speaking from Bangalore. My name is Ritam—Ritam Banerjee.'

'Yes, tell me. I'm Avik's father speaking.' Badshah's proper name was Avik.

'Uncle, I have some news. You do know that Avik was not keeping well?'

'Yes, I know. His right arm and leg were not functioning properly. He'd seen a doctor and he is on medication.' Sanjay replied.

'Yes, that's right. But the medicine wasn't working. So today we brought him to another hospital—I mean, to Columbia Asia. They have done an MRI here and it shows a tumour on his brain. Uncle, would you please speak to the doctor?' Ritam handed the phone to the doctor.

After speaking to the doctor, it became clear that due to the interim delay, the tumour had grown considerably. When Avik had gone to the other hospital—Manipal—about a week ago, the MRI should have been done. But instead, he had been prescribed some medicines which were of no use. Avik needed surgery immediately. Sanjay and Mili needed to go to Bangalore as soon as possible.

After the doctor finished speaking, Sanjay asked how soon was the surgery possible. The doctor said as soon as the parents were able to get there. Sanjay confirmed that they would reach the next day or the day after. He would start arranging for tickets in the morning. Thereafter he spoke to Ritam again, 'Ritam, I've got the details from the doctor. We are trying our best to reach there at the earliest. It is late in the night now. I shall arrange for the tickets tomorrow.'

Ritam said, 'Yes Uncle. Please speak to Avik.'

'Yes, hand him the phone please.'

Ritam passed the phone to Badshah. 'How are you, my son?' Sanjay asked.

Badshah sounded calm and collected, 'I'm okay, Baba. You and ma come here fast.'

'Yes dear, I'll try to reach tomorrow. You take care of yourself, son.' Sanjay's tone was threaded with nervous tension. All the others present there at the office were also listening to this conversation. They guessed parts of the story. Sanjay narrated it in brief to them after hanging up.

At the mention of brain tumour, Bhaskar said, 'This is becoming so prevalent nowadays. A man in our office had one. He went to Vellore and got it operated. After the surgery he did face some trouble with his left side. But physiotherapy helped and now he has joined work again, after three months. Sanjay-da, don't worry. Badshah will be absolutely fine.' Bhaskar was trying to provide moral support to Sanjay in this situation. He was in the Accounts department of Lafarge, the cement company. Bhaskar Upadhyay was very good at his work and he often helped out with many a task in the Building Society. He shared a good rapport with Sanjay.

Gopalan, who was sitting next to Bhaskar, said, 'Don't you worry. Columbia Asia is a good hospital. They have very good doctors. Your son will get well soon.'

A R Gopalan was the Treasurer of the Society. He was a Tamilian, but he spoke fluent Bengali. He had worked in Tata Steel for many years and retired a couple of years ago. The third person in the room was A K Roy. He was elderly and a man of few words. He too had been in Tata Steel, in Electrical. He handled all the technical tasks of the

Society. He lived on the floor above Sanjay and had known Badshah from when he was a baby. He asked Sanjay, 'Do you wish to go tomorrow?'

'Yes,' Sanjay said, 'I'll buy the tickets tomorrow. Let me see if I get a departure from Ranchi or Kolkata.'

Mr Roy's voice was soft as he replied, 'All right; don't worry about anything here. And if you need any help, do let me know.'

Jamshedpur did not have a civil airport. There was a tiny one that served Tata Steel, to ferry the executives to and fro Kolkata and Mumbai in chartered crafts. So if lay people from Jamshedpur wanted to catch a flight, they needed to travel a great distance, either to Ranchi or to Kolkata. For Ranchi one had to board the bus from Mango Bus Stand. It took three hours to reach Ranchi's Kantatoli. From there it was another tempo ride to the airport. And for Kolkata one had to take the train on a four-hour journey to Howrah station. The airport was a fair distance from Howrah. Lately, some air-conditioned buses had started plying between Howrah and Dumdum Airport. But since it wound its way through the city picking up passengers, it was a matter of a few more hours before one completed that journey.

Sanjay was pondering over all this when Arun said, 'Sanjay-da, via Ranchi will be the quickest. At this time, the sooner you reach the better it is. Arun Gadamshetty—the youngest of the seven directors of the Society. He was an officer in Tata Steel. Smart and competent, he hailed from Andhra Pradesh and was quite fluent in Hindi.

In the meantime, the hands of the clock had edged closer to ten. He needed to go home and talk to Mili. She knew nothing of all this. Surely Ritam had not called her. When he spoke of going home, the others too decided to lock up for the day and head home. Usually, the office used to be open until ten fifteen or ten thirty. Since the office was located within the colony, generally people frequented it until the late hours. The office opened up at around eight in the evening since everyone came home from work around seven or seven-thirty.

After shutting the office down, everyone headed to their own homes. The colony was fairly large. There were two hundred and eighty-five flats spread out in five phases. Sanjay, Bhaskar and Mr. Roy lived in Phase I. It was a bit far from the Society office, beside the main gate of the colony.

The three of them fell in step together. Guessing Sanjay's state of mind, Bhaskar began to give examples to illustrate that brain tumour was not a very grave danger these days, and how a lot of people contracted them and were subsequently cured.

When he reached home, he told Mili everything. She was extremely shocked and dejected. Brain tumour—Badshah had a brain tumour! She wanted to call Badshah immediately. Sanjay stopped her, 'Badshah is already admitted to the hospital. He does not have his mobile with him. Maybe you could call Ritam instead—Badshah's friend.'

Ritam tried to comfort Mili, 'Don't worry Aunty. It's just a tumour—surgery will fix it. There are very good doctors here. They will make it all right. But you and Uncle come here fast. Without you the surgery cannot happen.'

A mountain of anxiety pressed down upon Mili. How could this happen to Badshah? Just a few months ago, in December, she had visited him in Bangalore. Badshah had taken a flat for himself and he'd been asking her to come and stay with him. It was a one-bedroom apartment with a hall and a kitchen and he wanted to show it to his mother. Besides, there was some more shopping to be done for the house, for the kitchen and little curios. It would be easy to buy them with his mother's help.

Mili used to get the last week of December off from school. It was nearly a ten ten-day break and she used that to go to Bangalore. Sanjay had not gone. His mother was bedridden for the last three years. She was wheelchair-bound and needed help. There were attendants round the clock for her, but Sanjay and Mili could not leave the house to them and go away together. So, they had been visiting Badshah in Bangalore one by one, never together.

Mili had a whale of a time with her son. It was a pretty flat. The hall was large, though the room was a bit small. The kitchen was open-plan, but well laid out. Drinking water used to be delivered in a large jar. They just had to dial and it would be brought in. Badshah took five days off to spend time with his mother. Mili cooked his favourite dishes and one day she even invited two of his friends for a home-cooked meal. They watched great movies on his laptop. After lunch Badshah would suggest a movie and they would watch it together. His collection was truly exclusive: *Bicycle Thief*, *Dead Poets' Society*, such unique films. Mili enjoyed them thoroughly. She wondered at the kinds of subjects these films were made on! Her son'e taste was truly eclectic—not at all like other boys his age.

One evening Badshah said, 'Ma, come on, I'll take you to an art gallery. Rohan and Abhinav will also come. You will like it.' In the evening Rohan came over with Abhinav on his bike. Badshah and Mili hailed an autorickshaw. It was a brilliant gallery, with a fine display of art and sculpture both. There were Rabindranath Tagore, Abanindranath Tagore, Nandalal Bose, Ramkinkar Baij. Mili was awestruck with wonder. Badshah had wanted to take his mother to Nandi Hills. It was some distance from the city and an erstwhile summer retreat of Tipu Sultan. Since it was at a slight altitude, Nandi Hills was always a little cooler. It was a green oasis with hills all around—a very beautiful tourist spot indeed. Badshah had taken his father there and he remembered how pleased his father had been. He wanted to do the same for his mother. But he couldn't. Perhaps he couldn't arrange transport. Mili tried to console a disappointed Badshah by saying, 'If not this time, we'll do it the next time.'

Therefore, the gallery—was an attempt to find silver lining. After they left the place, Badshah asked, 'How did you like the art gallery, Ma?' Mili replied, 'Beautiful.' Badshah was pleased to bits. He had known Mili would like the place because his mother not only had a diploma in Kathak dance, but she was also an artist. The dance had been a rigorous training, but the art had been naturally honed.

That day Badshah had been very happy with his decision.

Suddenly Sanjay's words brought Mili down to earth, 'I'm arranging for tickets to fly day after tomorrow. You go to school tomorrow. There should be proper intimation before you take leave. Why don't you write out the leave application now? We'll take tomorrow evening's Jan Shatabdi to Kolkata.' Mili nodded. Then she called her daughter Ruhi and her son-in-law, Rajveer. They knew nothing. They lived in Gurgaon and Rajveer owned a small business.

Ruhi began to weep uncontrollably as soon as she heard it. She wanted to see her brother immediately. Rajveer tried to console her and calm her down. Finally, it was decided that the two of them would also try to reach Bangalore the day after tomorrow, i.e. 4 May. In the meantime, Bappa too had heard of it from Rintu. Bappa was the son of Partha, Sanjay's middle brother. He too lived in Gurgaon and was employed in a reputed NBFC (Non-Banking Financial Company). As soon as he heard it, Bappa spoke to Ruhi and decided to go to Bangalore. Bappa and Badshah had grown up together and they were very close. So Bappa decided to apply for leave the next day and head for Bangalore. He would try to book himself into the same flight as Ruhi and Rajveer.

The following day, 3 May, Sanjay and Mili took the train from Tatanagar station at around 5 pm, headed towards Howrah station. Partha would be at the station. They would spend the night at Partha's in Eden City complex. The flight to Bangalore was at 9.15 am the next day. They would reach their destination by 11.30 am. While they were in the train, Ruhi called. She, Rajveer and Bappa would reach Bangalore that very night. The flight tickets were booked.

Rajveer was from Rajasthan. His proper name was Vinod Singh Shekhawat. Their ancestral home was about a hundred kilometers from Jaipur. They owned quite a lot of land as well as two houses in Gurgaon. In addition, Rajveer's father had bought a large flat in Manesar. He had been in the Air Force. After retirement he had joined the private airline, Spice Jet, in a responsible position as Senior Maintenance Aircraft Engineer.

Ruhi and Rajveer had met in a gym. Later they grew close and fell in love. Nearly two years later, in 2015, on 9 March they got married legally. That too was quite unplanned and sudden. At the beginning of March Sanjay had said to Mili, 'Come on, let's visit Ruhi. We haven't gone to her in a while.'

Mili said, 'I'd have to apply for leave from school. There are no holidays now.'

Sanjay said, 'Do that. But there is a need to go.'

They reached Delhi via Ranchi. They met Rajveer at the Delhi airport. He came along with Ruhi, to pick them up. A very handsome young man—five feet nine inches tall, fair, a headful of thick hair, a fighting fit body.

Mili had been cajoling Ruhi to get married for quite some time. But Ruhi always replied that although Rajveer was willing, his family was not. And so he could not gather up the courage. Both Mili and Sanjay were unhappy about this. They worried about Ruhi's marriage. Neither did they get a chance to speak to Rajveer directly.

Now came the chance. That day Rajveer spent the entire day with them. In the evening Mili picked up the topic. Without beating about the bush Rajveer said that even if his family did not agree, he would go ahead with the marriage. Mili suggested, 'Now that we are here, it would be good to go ahead at this time.' Rajveer said it was possible three days later, on 9 March. A traditional marriage was not possible. But a civil marriage ceremony in court was an option. There was no need for advance notice. It would happen whenever they presented themselves in court.

That is what happened. On the morning of 9 March, around 10 am, Sanjay and Mili, along with Ruhi and Rajveer, headed for Ghaziabad. They were accompanied by Rahul, a friend of both Ruhi and Rajveer. Rahul had started a BPO with two other friends. Ruhi worked there. It was a well-paid job. Their primary target was to service the complaints of American clients and resolve them satisfactorily.

So Rahul—that giant shareholder of a small BPO—was going to Gaziabad to act as a witness in Ruhi and Rajveer's wedding. He had also arranged a lovely Innova car for the journey. Sanjay had also invited his old friends from Patna—Dhruv, Pana and Akhilesh along with their spouses. Akhilesh had some urgent work and could not come. His wife Sumana was present. Dhruv and Pana came with their wives.

There is an Arya Samaj marriage bureau very close to the Ghaziabad District Court. They conduct the Hindu marriage rites over there after the paperwork for the civil marriage was duly completed. The bride and groom exchanged garlands and also had a photo session. Thereafter, they escorted the party to the court and completed the registration process. It was all a matter of an hour and a half. No hassles. For twenty thousand or so, they took care of every detail.

Sanjay and Mili were delighted with the efficiency of the marriage bureau. They had no idea their daughter's wedding could be completed so smoothly and beautifully. Sanjay's friends and their families were very happy with the arrangements. They were all aware of Mili and Sanjay's concern and anxiety on the issue of Ruhi's marriage. After the civil ceremony, Sanjay treated everyone to a meal at a very nice restaurant. And then it was time for everyone to head home. Dhruv and Sunita invited Sanjay and Mili to their home before they went back. They all knew one another from their days together in Patna. The active politics over there had brought them all close to one another. Sunita and Dhruv shifted to Delhi and a few years later Sanjay was transferred to Jamshedpur. Now Mili and Sanjay accepted Sunita and Dhruv's invitation with alacrity.

The train took a bit longer to reach Kharagpur. Quite a few passengers had boarded the train at Jhargram. Kharagpur station had good tea available, which Sanjay had but Mili didn't. She was lost in thoughts of Badshah all the while. He had just turned twenty-seven. He had joined his new job barely three years ago. A couple of months ago he had even been promoted. Suddenly, what was this critical illness that had him in its grip? She was getting impatient to reach Bangalore and to see him.

After Kharagpur, the train picked up speed. It would not stop before Santragachhi. Janshatabdi was a fairly good train. Earlier it was called Shatabdi and it was fully air-conditioned. Later a few normal coaches were added and the word 'Jan', meaning common or lay, was added. It became accessible to the common man, who could not afford air-conditioned coaches.

Sanjay had often wondered, will there ever come a day when every person will be able to afford air-conditioned coaches? Will the class divide ever disappear? Wasn't that the goal of the Communist Party? This was but a tiny instance. Every aspect of life was strewn with divides and differences—be it income, food, wealth, clothes and shelter, health and education. Sanjay had spent a large number of years as a member of the Communist Party—from his student days to the end of his working life. Even after retirement he had joined the Party once again, albeit not too actively.

In truth, Sanjay had great faith in Marxism. He must have been twenty-two or twenty three when he first came in contact with it as a concept. In the early days, he had difficulty understanding 'dialectical materialism' and 'unity of opposites'. 'Quantitative' and 'Qualitative change' were of course easier to comprehend. It had been clearly explained in the Chemistry textbooks of eighth and ninth grades.

As he had grown older Sanjay read and understood more of Marxism and he became increasingly attracted to the concept. It was such a wondrous theory or philosophy. It could explain every phenomenon in the world—be it large or small. It could answer every 'why' and 'what' on earth. The sign of a true social science. Marxism has proved that society can also be governed by science and scientific laws. Of course, there were many doubts about the practical implementation of the hypothesis. And there were even more doubts about the paths adopted to find the answers to those questions. If scientific theories were not proven scientifically, they lost their scientific properties.

Sanjay had never been able to accept this human tendency of turning scientific inquiry into an unscientific process. Perhaps this was the reason why many people were reluctant to join the Communist Party. In the natural course of events, they would have signed up. But instead they have maintained a distance, and watched from afar, the doings of the Party. They have felt irritated, offended, and sometimes just pure hurt. Sanjay often felt the desire to pen down his thoughts on this unscientific exploration of a scientific inquiry.

The train was nearly reaching Santragacchi. Many people were at the exit, ready to disembark. It was convenient for many people to get off at Santragachhi and save on the time that the train took to reach Howrah from there. Often many long-distance trains were stalled in favour of local trains in the distance between Santragachhi and Howrah and that increased the travel time by at least half an hour.

Sanjay's mobile phone rang. It was Partha. He was waiting at Howrah station and he asked how far away they were. 'The train is just leaving Santragachhi,' as Sanjay spoke, the speed of the train dropped. Perhaps it was coming up against a red flag. 'There it goes,' Sanjay said to Partha, 'Let's see when it reaches.'

Partha said, 'No problem. I'll wait at the entrance to the platform.'

After crossing many signals, sometimes slowing down, stalling for a few minutes, the train puffed and huffed its way into Howrah station. It was nearly a quarter to ten in the night. As he'd promised, Partha was waiting at the spot where platform number nineteen just started. It was easy to spot him.

Sanjay and Mili reached him with their luggage in no time. Partha had bought a flat in Eden City. It was nearly ten kilometers from Taratala. From Howrah station it would usually be one and a half hours away. But since it was nighttime, it took a little less time. A flyover—from Jinjira Bazar to Batanagar—was under construction along the way. Since the construction work was underway on one side of the road, the other side was jammed with cars. This was the reason that it took a bit too long to reach Eden City, and that would be the state of affairs until the flyover was completed.

Partha was justifiably frustrated when he said, 'This construction is going on ever since we bought the flat. God knows when it will finish. People say by 2017 it should be complete.'

Sanjay said, 'Once it is complete, the situation will change. It will take a lot less time.' Mili agreed.

As soon as the cab entered Eden City, their mood lifted. A huge gate was manned by alert, young security guards dressed in smart uniforms. The roads were wide, well-laid, and tree-lined. A little ahead there was a huge playground, bordered by a swimming pool, gymnasium, a departmental store and a guest house. Partha mentioned that there was even an air-conditioned restaurant on the first floor of the building. It was nothing short of fabulous.

This was Sanjay and Mili's first visit to Partha's new home. It was only in last September that Partha and his family left Jamshedpur and came here.

Since it was quite late at night, they finished dinner and retired early. The next morning, they would have to leave the house at seven-thirty. The flight was at nine-thirty.

Partha had instructed his driver—Gaur. He would drive them to the airport.

They reached the airport within time to catch flight the next morning. The roads were emptier in the morning and the flyover work had not yet begun for the day. So, Gaur drove rather fast and brought the car to a halt in front of the Departure gate. Sanjay got down and unloaded the luggage from the trunk of the car. Partha and Gaur drove away. Before he left, Partha said, 'Give me Badshah's news as soon as you reach there.'

Partha doted on Badshah. Ever since he was a little boy, Partha reposed great faith in Badshah's intelligence. The four cousins—Ruhi, Bappa, Bonnie, and Badshah—were a few years apart in age. Of the four, Badshah was the best in Math. He would solve complicated sums mentally. There was a tutor in the Shonari region of Jamshedpur called Bashu-da. He was Bappa and Badshah's tutor and he would always claim that Badshah had a good head for Mathematics.

Moreover, Badshah was always very good-natured. He would quietly do his studies and never disturb a soul. In fact, from a very young age, he would get ready for school entirely on his own. He did not need any help. He would get dressed, pick up his school bag, take his Dadu's (grandfather's) fingers and head for the bus stop with his little feet. It was a sight to see—the tiny Badu hanging onto his five-feet-eleven-inches tall Dadu's fingers and heading for the bus stop. His Dadu always called him Badu.

It was the same story when he came back from school. Dadu would leave the house at the correct time, and wait for him at the bus stop. The moment the bus came to a halt, Badu would rush helter-skelter in his hurry to get off. The tiny legs trying to take those high steps often caused him difficulty, but his eagerness lent his feet wings. On the last step his patience would snap and he would throw himself directly onto Dadu's chest.

Dadu was no less. He was always there to catch his catapulting grandson, his tall arms spread wide in welcome. The sight of Badu's unflinching trust as he launched himself in the air towards Dadu, and the infinite love and pride with which Dadu received him into his arms was a sight for sore eyes. Every day the conductor of the bus and all the other children in it enjoyed this spectacle as if it was happening for the first time.

Sanjay and Mili cleared the Security Check and boarded the flight. The flight attendant was already explaining the safety and emergency guidelines. The plane would soon be in the air—on time.

3

15 JULY

•••

Patna—15 July 1988. It was eight in the night when Mili had her labour pains. Even after some time, the pain showed no sign of abating. Sanjay's mother said, 'I think she needs to be hospitalized.' Sanjay's grandmother concurred with her. 'This doesn't feel like a false alarm,' she said. Grandmother obviously had the greatest experience of these things. She had witnessed many childbirth in her lifetime and knew how to tell a genuine labour pain apart from a false alarm. Hence, Sanjay started the preparations for going to the hospital. Partha was at home. He went to fetch Shubai, the rickshaw-wallah. Shubai had his own rickshaw. There was a slum close to the house. Most rickshaw pullers, cart vendors, construction workers and many other people from the labourer class lived there. In the local language it was called a Jhuggi Jhopri. It was on the left-hand side of the road that ran between Bahadurpur and Rajendranagar. Right behind the Jhuggi Jhopri was the PG Hostel, which housed the students who came to Patna to pursue their Masters from other cities of the country.

Shubai lived in the Jhopri. He was a great fan of Sanjay's father. In Patna the middle-class and lower middle-class people resorted to the rickshaw as their sole mode of transport. Whenever Sanjay's father needed to go somewhere, Shubai would bring his rickshaw to the doorstep.

Partha fetched Shubai now, to take Mili to PMCH in his rickshaw. Mili had already changed and was ready to go. Sanjay's mother packed a bag with the necessary things for a hospital stay, and handed it to Sanjay. Along with Mili, Sanjay set off for the Patna Medical College Hospital. Partha followed them on his bike. It was nearly nine in the night. The sky was overcast with dark clouds.

The maternity ward of PMCH was extremely unclean. The entire hospital was the same. But this ward was even more so. At first, Mili was a bit uncomfortable. She was from Jamshedpur, where things were different. First because it was an industrial town. But also because it had natural beauty, especially Telco. The touch of the mountains and vast tracts of green lent a special kind of beauty to Telco.

Although Mili was born in her maternal home in Uttarpara, she was raised entirely in Telco, where her father worked. Badshah's sister Ruhi, their first child, was born in the Telco Hospital. Mili's brother, Tablu, worked in Telco. In a tragic accident in 1979, Mili's father had lost his life in the factory in Telco. That was how Tablu was given the job. As per the Telco rules, Mili had the opportunity to get admitted into their hospital. It was only to be availed for the birth of the first child. Mili could still remember vividly the neat and clean environs of that hospital.

They eventually got a cabin in PMCH. It was quite clean. The equipment may not have been the most modern, but it was a decent setup. Sanjay was relieved. In a short while, a female doctor came and examined Mili. She prescribed a few essential medicines and assured them, 'There's no need to worry. All is well.'

Partha went to fetch the medicines from the pharmacy that was just outside the PMCH gates. At the time there wasn't a pharmacy within the compound of the hospital. If you stepped out of the main gate or any of the other gates, you would directly walk on the most important highway of Patna—Ashok Rajpath. All the colleges under Patna University were strewn around Ashok Rajpath. It was the busiest road in the city. Pataliputra was the erstwhile capital of the Magadha Empire and modern-day Patna did not forget to salute and honour that feather in its cap. The highway was named after the Emperor of Magadha who had seized the throne after killing his ninety-nine brothers and then after a display of extreme and violent valour in the battle of Kalinga, the same Emperor had a change of heart so complete that he was transformed into a non-violent proponent of the Buddhist faith. His role in the spread of Buddhism is written in golden letters on the pages of history.

This highway was lined with shops selling books, clothes, sweets, medicines—every conceivable need that man could have. Partha fetched the prescribed medicines from one of these shops.

Meanwhile, everyone else had gone back home. Mili's mother and Sanjay's father were dying to go to the hospital. Mili's mother had arrived in Patna a few weeks ago, in anticipation of her daughter's delivery date in mid-July. When Mili was leaving for the hospital, her mother wanted to come along. But Sanjay's father said, 'Let them go ahead. We shall join them in a while.' Shubai had been instructed accordingly. Therefore, Shubai went back to the house that same night. Sanjay's father and Mili's mother were ready to leave. It had started raining by then. Big, fat raindrops. The sky was laden with frowning dark clouds. Within minutes there was waterlogging in the streets. As the level of water rose, Shubai's rickshaw slowed down incrementally. The two elderly people huddled into the seat as Shubai pulled the old rickshaw with all his might, hauling it towards the destination. They reached PMCH past midnight.

Partha was waiting for them at the entrance of the maternity ward. He escorted them to the cabin where

Sanjay was already seated. Mili's pains had shot up further. Mili's mother pulled up a chair, sat down and began to stroke Mili's brow. Sanjay's father proceeded to the waiting area.

A little before two in the night the pain began to shoot up. Two nurses came and checked on Mili. Shortly a midwife came into the room. The arrangements for the delivery were underway. Sanjay and Mili's mother had to leave the cabin.

They could hear Mili weeping in the room. The midwife was also heard giving instructions to the nurses. The nurses were murmuring amongst themselves. Sanjay was pacing the floor right outside the cabin. Mili's mother stood in a corner of the corridor with a face lined with worry and concern.

Suddenly—the sound of an infant weeping. Mili's cries had gone silent. The wise and experienced midwife wounded delighted. The younger nurses were also thrilled. A healthy, beautiful baby was born—fair complexion, a tiny sharp nose, bright eyes with a twinkle in them, two red shapely lips, brows the shape of bows and a headful of thick black hair. Badshah's eyes were open from the minute he was born. He was taking everything in, his eyes full of curiosity for this world he had come into. He would have to live here, face many hardships, battle many hurdles, and of course, love all the people around him, love the world, the entire planet.

Badshah was born at five minutes past two in the morning. By the Gregorian calendar that would be 15 July 1988. Mili's mother hurtled into the cabin. First, she checked on Mili. There were tears in Mili's eyes, her face bore the traces of pain. The two nurses looked a little worried, even amidst their joy. The midwife too looked a little concerned. There seemed to be a slight complication. Mili's mother was delighted to see the baby. But her concern over Mili's condition grew by the minute. At that late hour there were no senior doctors present. So, the junior doctor was informed. He took a look and said that a minor surgery was required. Mili was prepared for the OT. In the meantime, Sanjay's father and Partha had also come into the cabin. The midwife handed the baby to Mili's mother. Badshah continued to scan everything around him with curious eyes, as he lay in his grandmother's arms. Everyone present were all eyes for the beautiful baby. It was pouring cats and dogs outside. That night Patna was nearly flooded. In a short while Mili came back from the OT. She was fine now. Mili's mother gently placed Badshah next to Mili. As she looked at Sanjay, the tears flowed unchecked from Mili's eyes. Sanjay's eyes mirrored hers. These were tears of joy.

Slowly, the ferocity of the downpour abated. The sky grew clearer before daybreak. A little later the eastern sky was tinged with scarlet. 15 July 1988 gifted everyone a bright new morning.

4

COLUMBIA ASIA

...

They landed in Bangalore by half past eleven in the morning. By the time they left the airport it was noon. There were rows of cabs right outside the terminal—Ola or Uber and many other kinds. Most of them charged by the meter and some were prepaid, according to the distance of the destination. After some deliberation, they decided to go with a cab. Some haggling got them a rate of seven hundred for passage to the Columbia Asia hospital in Yeshwantpur. There were two hospitals by the same name in Bangalore. One was in Yeshwantpur and the other in Hebbal. Badshah was in the former.

Sanjay had said, 'Let's go home first. We can dump our luggage there and then go to the hospital.' But Mili did not agree. She said, 'No, let us go to the hospital directly. Luggage is not a problem; we can keep them with us in the hospital.' So, they headed straight for the hospital. The Bangalore roads were in good condition, smooth and wide. But the traffic was a nightmare everywhere. It took a little over an hour to reach the hospital. As they paid the cab and stepped in through the main gate, they ran into Ruhi, Rajveer and Bappa, their nephew. Mili had given them the heads up on the phone and so they were at the gate.

Bappa said, 'Theu, come, let's do a brainstorming among ourselves before we meet Badshah.' Bappa's name for Sanjay was 'Theu'. All his nephews and nieces from his brothers called Sanjay that. It was an abbreviation of Jetheu or paternal uncle who was older than one's father. It was a name given by Sanjay's mother, or their grandmother. There were more, such as Chhotka for youngest uncle and Mejka for second uncle.

Sanjay replied, 'All right, let's sit somewhere.' Since they had come the day before, Bappa and the others had already spoken to the doctor and they'd also seen the MRI report. They all sat down on two sofas facing one another in the spacious lounge on the ground floor. Bappa spoke first, 'Look, we've seen both the plate and the report of the MRI. The tumour has grown considerably. It needs immediate surgery. the MRI should have happened sooner. Anyway, now that you two are here, the surgery should go through as soon as possible. They are ready for tomorrow. They just need your consent. Chhotka will also be here soon. I've spoken to him on the phone.'

Rajveer said, 'It'll be possible to meet the doctor and speak to him at around four in the evening.'

Mili was getting very impatient by now, 'Come on, let us go to Badshah. I want to see him.'

Ruhi said, 'Come, it's cabin number seven on the third floor.'

Everyone proceeded to Badshah's cabin. Badshah was beside himself on seeing his parents. He almost shot out of the bed and onto his feet. Mili hugged him tight and caressed him lovingly. 'How are you, my dear?' She asked with love and concern. Badshah's voice carried his supreme sense of security as he said, 'I'm fine. Now that you two are here—everything will be all right.'

Then Sanjay hugged Badshah and he reciprocated. He held on to Sanjay like a lifeline. 'Baba, how are you?' Badshah asked. The question carried the utter bliss of receiving a great gift, rather than any anxiety. It was the pleasure of getting his father close at last, and the supreme confidence that now all would be well.

Sanjay said, 'I am fine, son. How are you?' and he kissed Badshah's brow.

'I am fine now. You are here. Now my surgery can proceed.' Badshah said it with a trusting smile.

Rohan and Ritam were also present there. Rohan was known to them all from his childhood. He was from

Jamshedpur and had studied in Loyola, not in Rajendra Vidyalay as Badshah had. They had met on the football field, both being aficionados. They would often visit each other's home.

Ritam was a colleague of Badshah. Both of them worked in an American multinational company. This was the same boy who had called Sanjay on the night of 2 May and informed him about Badshah's condition. It was he who brought Badshah to Columbia Asia and he was the reason that Badshah's treatment was now on the correct course. As Ritam tried to touch Sanjay's feet respectfully, the latter drew him into his arms. That embrace carried a deep sense of gratitude and the warmth of closeness.

Mili was speaking to Rohan. Badshah drew her attention, 'Ma, this is Ritam. He is my friend from the office and he brought me here to this hospital.' Ritam bent low to touch Mili's feet, and like Sanjay, she too raised him affectionately and asked, 'Where is your home? How long have you been in Bangalore?'

'About three years now. Avik and I started working at the same time. My home is in Kolkata, in Howrah.'

By then Ruhi and Rajveer had brought some food for Mili and Sanjay, from the canteen upstairs. Sandwiches and coffee. They ate with gusto because they were hungry. Bappa went down to meet Rintu and bring him up.

Since the wedding, Rajveer tried to follow Bengali closely and he could, to some extent. But between themselves Ruhi and Rajveer spoke in Hindi. Since Ruhi had studied in Delhi, her spoken Hindi was as good as her English. Her twelve years in Delhi had given her a good grip on the intonations and nuances of Hindi. Rajveer of course, was familiar with it by birth. So, there were no language barriers between Ruhi and Rajveer and she did not want to pressurize Rajveer to learn Bengali.

Bappa returned to the cabin with Rintu, who kept his tiny suitcase in a corner and rushed to Badshah. Rintu's arrival made Badshah very happy. Rintu leaned over and hugged Badshah, 'How are you, my dear?'

Badshah's voice was laced with joy and confidence, 'I am fine Chhotka. How are you?' Badshah had immense faith in his Chhotka. This was true of all the four cousins—the children of Sanjay and Partha. All of them had done their higher studies in Delhi. At the time Rintu lived in Noida, adjoining Delhi. Bappa, Ruhi, Badshah, Bonnie had often dropped in one of their Chhotka in those days. They had all reaped the benefits of Chhotka's car, some more and some less. Each of them reposed great faith in the presence of Chhotka. Today Badshah's voice carried that faith. The anxiety of a brain tumour showing up in the MRI was overridden with a feeling of contented confidence, now that Chhotka was here. It was stamped on Badshah's face.

Bappa and Rajveer went in search of the surgeon. Dr. Raghuraman—well known in his field. He would do the surgery. He was already in the hospital. Bappa wanted to get his Theu and Chhotka to speak to the surgeon. In the meantime, Ruhi had brought tea and biscuits from the canteen, 'Chhotka, have this first.' She knew that Chhotka was very fond of tea. After drinking his tea, Chhotka, along with Bappa and Rajveer, headed for the surgeon's chamber.

First, they met the junior doctors. They informed them that the surgery was quite complicated and time-consuming. There was a risk element, naturally—it was a brain surgery after all.

In a short while Dr Raghuraman arrived. Tall and athletic, wheatish complexion, he had a commanding presence. Once the introductions were complete, he said, 'See, the sooner we do the surgery, the better it is. For various reasons, there has been a lot of delay already.'

Rintu asked, 'Doctor, we heard that the tumour has grown a bit. Will it be possible to extract all of it?'

'Haven't you seen the MRI plates?' Dr Raghuraman asked Rintu.

'I haven't had the time yet; they have seen it.'

Bappa and Rajveer had both seen it. Bappa said, 'Yes sir, I have seen it. The tumour is really quite large.' Rajveer nodded in agreement.

Dr. Raghuraman said, 'See, the challenge is in extracting as much of the tumour as possible and yet prevent as much damage to Avik's system as is possible. If you touch the brain, chances are it will affect some organ or the other. Since the tumour is on the left side of Avik's brain, the surgery will affect his right side. That means the right leg and the right arm. His speech will also be affected. But physiotherapy should be able to recover most of it.' Dr Raghuraman was naturally referring to Badshah as Avik since that was the name on the hospital register. And they did not know his nickname—Badshah.

After hearing him out, Rintu said, 'So sir, you'll have to be progressive on one hand and conservative on the other.'

Dr Raghuraman smiled, 'Exactly.'

Bappa asked, 'How long do you think the surgery will take?'

Dr Raghuraman said, 'At least seven to eight hours. But it depends on the patient. If there is excessive bleeding, then it will take longer. As they finished talking, they started walking back to Badshah's cabin. Before they parted, Rintu said to the doctor, 'We have no words at present. We can only hope and pray that the surgery is successful.'

Dr Raghuraman smiled and replied, 'Certainly.'

As evening approached, Badshah's friends started dropping by. Some were from ISBM, or International School for Business and Media, who had been with him during the MBA. The campus was about forty kilometers away from Bangalore. It had a branch in Pune which was quite renowned. Thereafter, the Bangalore branch was started in 2010 in the village of Nirubanda. Badshah's batch was the second one. When Sanjay and Mili had gone to get Badshah admitted, the building was still incomplete. The admission office was open in a makeshift building on the right, just after one entered the gates. There were a few more rooms with it, and a huge common hall. Sandeep was also there, along with Sanjay, Mili and Badshah. Sandeep was Badshah's childhood friend. They had studied in the same school in Jamshedpur. Sandeep's father worked at Tata Steel. When he discovered that they were getting Badshah admitted to ISBM in Bangalore, he too spoke to Badshah and decided to get Sandeep admitted there. One big reason for this decision was that Sandeep too wished the same. Truth be told, Sandeep was not just a very close friend of Badshah, he was also a great fan of Badshah's intelligence and charm. At the time of admission, therefore, both Sandeep and Badshah were very happy.

When they heard of Badshah's hospitalization, Sandeep, Rupak, Rajesh, Abhinav, Aparajita, and a few others from ISBM dropped in. There were visitors from his office as well. Then there were his friends with whom he played football every weekend. Most of them were very tall—five feet eleven, five feet ten or even a full six feet tall. Badshah was not that tall. He was five feet four inches in all. Sanjay and Mili were tearful as they watched their small-built son being encouraged, and empathized with by a bunch of youngsters who towered over him. As Sanjay was stepping out of the cabin to hide his tears, he heard one of them speak with great emotion, 'Avik, tu theek ho ja jaldi, aur sun, jab takt u theek nahi hoga, hum log koi football nahi khelenge.' (Avik, hurry up and get well, and until you get well, none of us will play football.)

At this, Badshah turned to one side and began to weep silently. One of the boys went and grabbed his right hand tightly in his fist. It was impossible for Sanjay to stay there after this. He wanted to go away and weep in a secluded corner—tears of joy, so grateful was he for the love that was being showered on his son. Sanjay was well aware of how addicted sportsmen were to their game. And yet, a footballer was saying, 'Avik, tu theek ho ja jaldi, aur sun, jab takt u theek nahi hoga, hum log koi football nahi khelenge.' How much love and affection had to be there, for a footballer to say this to another.

Sanjay himself had played some football in his youth. Sanjay's father was a well-known footballer in the Kolkata Maidan. Therefore, the true import of such a vow was not unknown to Sanjay. Tears streamed down his cheeks as he gazed lovingly at his son. He wondered how blessed was this boy, what was the charm that drew others to him like a magnet.

When he had been introduced to the tall athletes, Sanjay had come to know that some of them were Muslims, some Hindus and some Christians. Amongst Badshah's office colleagues, most were from South India, some were North Indians and some were Bengalis too. From the expression of worry, anxiety and concern that he had spotted on all their faces, one thing was clear to Sanjay: Badshah was very dear to them. That was why one of those towering athletes took Sanjay's hand as he was leaving, and said, 'Uncle, your son is a gem of a person.'

Sanjay took it all in with his ears and eyes. And he wondered that he never knew of this quality in his son. He knew that his son was polite, sweet-natured, full of curiosity, quick on the uptake, always gave more importance to knowledge than to grades in exams—and his son was crazy about sports, especially football. That was dearer to him than life itself. He could give up everything for football. Sanjay knew all this about his son. But he did not know that his son had, over the years, taken so many people to his heart and become so dear to so many people. Sanjay looked at Mili with wonder in his eyes.

Mili was in a similar state. She gazed back at Sanjay with the same wonder in her eyes. The parents had joy and contentment stamped on their faces. Amid the gloom in their minds, a bolt of happiness shot through. In the evening the news arrived that Arnab was on his way over. Arnab was another childhood friend of Badshah. He had grown up in the same colony in Jamshedpur. At present he is working in Delhi. He had spoken to Rohan a few times on the phone and come to know that Badshah had a crucial surgery the following day. So, he was on his way to Bangalore, to encourage Badshah and boost his morale.

As the evening wore on, the crowd grew thicker and faster in Badshah's cabin. The security staff on the third floor were, by then, well aware of Avik Roy and his cabin number. Despite all their attempts, they could not stem the flow of Badshah's visitors. The two helpless security personnel were forced to accept defeat in the face of a crowd that strong. They did try to inform the hospital authorities once. But there was no interest from above in controlling the number of visitors in Avik Roy's cabin; on the contrary, there seemed to be a covert indulgence. A boy at the peak of his youth, twenty-seven years old—his number of friends was countless, he had a tumour in his brain—the next day his surgery was scheduled and thereafter the tumour would go for a biopsy, no one knew what would be the outcome. With all these factors in mind, perhaps even the hospital authorities were too overwhelmed to spout rules and discipline.

Badshah was delighted to see so many people milling around him. Everyone was of the same mind—there was no need to worry, the surgery would be successful, the tumour would be extracted, all will be well—these surgeries were commonplace today.

Badshah was at a loss for words to respond to so many people saying so many things. He wore a smile of reassurance and kept repeating, 'Don't worry, I am not afraid—I will be fine.'

The evening was gradually wearing into night. Now the security staff began to nudge the visitors towards the hands of the clock. Patients had been served their dinner. Very slowly, the crown in the cabin began to thin out. Everyone decided they will all be back by ten in the morning. An hour after that Badshah would be wheeled into the OT. Before that some forms would have to be signed. Rintu had already had a word with the nurses.

Now they picked up their luggage and Sanjay, Mili, Rintu and Ruhi got into a cab and headed for Badshah's flat. Rajveer and Bappa got into a cab with Monica, Badshah's friend. She lived in Banaswadi, in the same complex as Badshah, just one floor below. It was quite late in the night when they reached the flat. Mili and Ruhi freshened up and began to organize dinner. It was difficult—organizing a meal for so many people in an unfamiliar kitchen. Besides, everyone was famished.

Mili said to Ruhi, 'Just check if there are eggs in the fridge. Otherwise, ask Rajveer to get a dozen eggs from downstairs. I saw on my way here that a shop is open.' There were no eggs in the fridge. Ruhi said to Rajveer, 'Please go and get a dozen eggs from the shop downstairs.' Rajveer complied. Mili had boiled some lentils along with the rice. With some eggs, the simple meal of boiled rice and daal went down well with everyone. Then they began to discuss matters of importance.

Rintu said, 'Let us discuss the finances. I'm sure Badshah has medical insurance. How much is that? And does anyone have an estimate of the cost of surgery?'

Sanjay said, 'I have heard from Badshah that he is insured for about four lakhs. And the estimate is of three lakhs and seventy-five thousand.'

Bappa said, 'Yes, that is correct. But Chhotka, the actual bill will be of a much higher amount, because they do not cover everything in the estimate. Besides, for certain categories of spend, there is a ceiling from Mediclaim, it would not cover beyond a certain amount. So, we must have some cash in hand.'

Sanjay said, 'I do have some cash handy.'

Bappa and Rintu said the same. So, for the moment they were covered. After the surgery, they would have to look at the situation once again and take stock afresh.

Now the sleeping arrangements. Mili and Ruhi went downstairs to sleep in Monica's flat. Sanjay, Rintu, Rajveer and Bappa spent the night in Badshah's flat. There was enough room to go around. In the morning, everyone set off by eight thirty. Two cabs made a beeline for Columbia Asia. They needed to reach by ten. But they overshot the mark by a few minutes. The traffic situation in Bangalore was really abysmal. Gone were the days when Kolkata was considered the worst in this regard. The next in line after Bangalore was perhaps Mumbai. Sometimes Delhi too edged its way past. But Bangalore ruled the roost with its burgeoning vehicles and growing traffic jams. Over the last two decades Bangalore had witnessed phenomenal growth in the IT sector. It had attracted thousands of young men and women from all over India, with unbounded employment opportunities being the prime draw. Hence the growth in population, in traffic, and traffic snarls.

When they reached the hospital, the doctor had already arrived. As they stepped into Badshah's cabin a nurse informed them that they were needed in the office, to sign some forms. Rintu and Bappa headed for the office. A tiny barricaded space went by the name of the office. One nonmedical staff sat there with a junior. As they stepped in, the staff member handed some forms to Rintu and Bappa. This was a declaration to be signed before the surgery that in case of a negative outcome, the hospital would not be held responsible. They filled out the form and took Sanjay's signature at the bottom. In the meantime, many friends and colleagues of Badshah had already arrived. Badshah was his usual self, speaking to everyone with a pleasant smile. He was unfed since the morning. A surgery required one to be fasting.

In a short while two ward boys came into the cabin. They were going to take Badshah to the OT. In a flash, was that a shadow of fear that Sanjay saw passing over Badshah's face? But he had himself in check immediately. Everyone continued to encourage him—some were shaking his hands, some were stroking his arms, and some were just shouting positive assertations. Badshah headed for the OT on his stretcher. A horde of people were following the stretcher. A nurse saw this and said to Badshah, 'Avik, look how many people are there for you. Tell me one thing: what do you do, where do you live?' Pat came his reply, 'In the hearts of people.' The stretcher was slowly wheeled into the OT. Badshah disappeared from everyone's sight.

5

SURGERY

•••

Everyone waited with a mountain of anxiety. Nearly six and a half hours had elapsed. They still hadn't brought Badshah out of the OT. Did that mean he was not well? Was the operation unsuccessful? Could they extract the tumour from the brain? Or did Badshah's other organs get affected in the process? Each of the people present there had such a whirl of thoughts swirling within them, although one message did arrive on Bappa's phone: 'patient is doing well; no profuse bleeding so far.'

The message had come from one of the junior doctors present in the OT. They had intimated them before going into the OT that a message would come soon after they began the surgery. Just after making the incision in the skull, if there was excessive bleeding, it was a reason for concern. In that situation proceeding with the surgery becomes a challenge. In the absence of that the prognosis was better. This was the message imparted to the patient's family usually. That is why they had taken Bappa's phone number.

But many hours had passed since that message came in at around noon. It was now half past five in the evening. No further intimation had come. Everyone was impatient and concerned. Rintu went ahead to inquire at the little desk where a nurse was sitting. He asked her, 'The patient of cabin number seven is in the OT. Is everything all right?' The nurse replied, 'I'm sure it is. Avik, right? There hasn't been any news so far. You know what they say—no news…good news.' She smiled.

Rintu said, 'That is true. But it has been many hours.'

The nurse said, 'Please wait a bit longer. I shall try and find out.'

Rintu went back to the waiting area.

A doctor stepped out of the OT at half past six and informed them that the operation was successful. The patient was doing well. In a short while he would be transferred to the CCU, when people would be able to meet him, one by one.

Since it was already evening, the crown in waiting had started swelling. Those who had not been able to come in the morning due to work, had also started drifting in. There was some excitement about who would go in to see

Badshah first. After some discussion the following lineup was decided on: Ma, Baba, Didi, Chhotka, Bappa, Monica...followed by friends. Accordingly, Mili stepped into the CCU first. There was a corridor and then on the left a mid-sized ward. All around were patients, some unconscious, some half-conscious. Some wore an oxygen mask and some were on drip. Mili could not spot Badshah in their midst. Finally she asked the nurses and was told that he was in one of the cabins towards one end of the ward.

Mili went in. Badshah had regained a considerable amount of consciousness. He could recognize her immediately. His head was swathed in bandage. His left had had the saline drip attached to it. The railing guards around his bed were all raised.

He tried to speak, 'M-m-m-maah.' Not much came out. Just the sounds of M-m-m-m-mma came out. Mili could tell that he was having difficulty speaking. She was aware that a brain surgery affected other faculties, including speech. Mili thought, 'Will he never be able to speak again?' Tears welled up in her eyes. She checked them with all her might and said, 'See, you could recognize me all right! You'll be able to speak too, child—gradually. Everything will be all right. My darling son!'

She stroked his arms and caressed him with all her love for a few minutes and then came away, after telling him, 'I am sending Baba. He is waiting outside.'

No Sanjay went in. He recognized Sanjay as well. But all he could say was that same 'M-m-m-maah.' Sanjay couldn't help saying, 'Badu, it's me, Baba? Do you recognize me?'

Badshah still said, 'M-m-m-maah.' Now Sanjay understood that Badshah was unable to form the words that he wanted to utter. All he could say was 'M-m-m-maah.' This was not his speech. As he tried to speak, this was the only sound he could make, almost by default.

The same worries began to take shape in Sanjay's mind, as had in Mili's. Would Badshah ever be able to speak again? He had his entire life in front of him. Would he have to go through his life verbally challenged? Sanjay's heart twisted in his chest. But he couldn't weep in front of Badshah. Nothing could be done here, which could potentially break his spirit. He was already in a great deal of pain. If his spirit was broken in addition to the physical pain, he would never heal. Despite all his inner turmoil and fears, Sanjay concealed everything from Badshah and somehow came away from the CCU.

In the same way, Ruhi, Rintu and Monica went and visited Badshah. He responded to each one of them. Perhaps he recognized all of them too. But his lips could only utter 'M-m-m-maah.'

That night Badshah remained in the CCU. The next morning, he was shifted to a cabin at ten. By then, his speech had cleared up a little. He could now say Baba. Although he still could not speak completely legibly, it was reasonably better than the night before. At this everyone felt happier. Mili and Sanjay were extremely glad. Badshah was speaking many words quite clearly, putting all their fears to rest. But now another challenge presented itself—Badshah's right leg and arm were not functional. Despite all attempts, Badshah could not move his right limbs at all. He was looking visibly disturbed at this turn of events. The nurse came and informed them that Dr Raghuraman would come to see Badshah shortly.

The doctor came a little past eleven. He spoke at length with Badshah. He motivated Badshah to continue to speak. Badshah tried, but most of his words were unclear. He could not answer all the questions. The doctor assured them that in a few days' time Badshah would be able to speak almost as before. But his right limbs will take time to get back in shape. Since his brain surgery took place on the left lobe, his right side was affected. The brain worked diagonally in that sense—the left lobe controlled the right side and vice versa. Physiotherapy will gradually restore functions to the limbs. He prescribed physiotherapy and speech therapy the following day.

He then asked Rintu to step outside the cabin for a moment. The doctor said to Rintu, 'See, speech or the use of limbs will come back gradually over time. But the real issue is elsewhere. The tumour sample has been sent for biopsy. The report is expected within three or four days. That will tell us whether it is malignant or not. If it is malignant, we have cause to worry.'

Rintu asked, 'Sir, what do you feel? What are the chances of it being malignant?'

Dr Raghuraman replied, 'Quite high.'

There was a huge canteen on the third floor. It served south Indian and north Indian food. It wasn't cheap, but neither did it burn a hole in the pocket. It was always crowded. Everyone ate there, starting from relatives of patients to the doctors, nurses, and other hospital staff. From breakfast to dinner, the place was always chockful of people.

Sanjay and the others had eaten breakfast and lunch at this same canteen on the day of the surgery as well as on the next day. Only their dinners were eaten in Badshah's flat. This caused a bit of pressure on the purse, naturally.

Two days later Rintu brought it up, 'How about we eat breakfast at home, before coming here?'

Everyone agreed. But there was one stumbling block: if they had to leave after breakfast, it would be at least nine o' clock before they could be out of the house. The journey to the hospital would take a minimum of one and a half hours. Wouldn't it be difficult if they reached the hospital at ten thirty or even later? Usually, the doctors started visiting somewhat by nine . Finally, after much discussion they decided that one of them should reach the hospital by nine. Rintu volunteered to do it.

The next day, 7 May, Rintu reached the hospital before nine. Badshah was now able to speak a little better. He wished Rintu 'Good Morning' as soon as he saw him. Rintu responded happily and he called Sanjay to inform him of the same.

At night Rohan had stayed with Badshah. Rintu asked him, 'Did you sleep well at night? Did Avik sleep fine?' Rohan knew Badshah as Avik. They had studied in different schools. But they were bosom buddies. The joy that Badshah felt on seeing Rohan, was unmatched. It was the same for Rohan. When the two of them visited Jamshedpur together, they would spend half the day together, every day.

Rohan had come over with two changes of clothes, to stay with Badshah in the hospital. And he had brought his laptop. He was scheduled to write his Civil Services exam in a few days. He was a good student. If he worked at it, he could easily clear this exam. But he refused to leave Badshah's side. He wouldn't budge from the hospital.

Rohan's presence made Badshah quite cheerful. Perhaps that was the reason he had slept well at night. Rintu noticed Rohan's fondness for Badshah. So, he asked indulgently, 'Don't you want to go home? I am here. You can go home for a while.' Rohan replied, 'No uncle, I won't go. I'll stay with Avik.' Rintu looked at Badshah. His face wore a look of contentment and approval. He couldn't speak at will. But if he could, he would perhaps have said, 'Let him be, let Rohan stay with me. He will be quite comfortable here. He will also study for his exams here.'

Rintu desisted from speaking. Instead, he picked up the intercom and placed an order for two cups of tea, for himself and for Rohan. He asked Rohan, 'Have you eaten?'

Rohan said, 'No. I'll just go to the canteen and have a bite.'

'Let me ask for a sandwich for you.' Rintu placed the order on the intercom. The next moment Dr Raghuraman entered the room.

He asked Badshah, 'Avik, how are you?'

Badshah replied, 'Fine.'

'Good,' the doctor was happy. 'From today Avik's physiotherapy will start, all right?'

Badshah nodded. After greeting the doctor, Rintu asked him, 'Sir, do we get the report today?'

'Let me check. If it has come, you'll be informed immediately.' The doctor left.

The tea and sandwich arrived from the canteen. Half an hour later Sanjay and the rest of the family too arrived. They all hugged and caressed Badshah. Rajveer and Bappa shook hands with him.

A little later a portly lady came in. She shook Badshah's hand and said, 'Avik, I am Dr Shibani, the physiotherapist. Dr. Raghuraman has instructed that I do the physiotherapy with you. Are you ready?'

Badshah nodded.

Dr. Shibani said, 'In that case you'll have to come to our Rehabilitation Room. It is on the second floor. I shall send the wheelchair. You can come in that.' She then glanced at Mili and asked, 'Would one of you like to come with him?'

Within ten minutes a ward boy wheeled in the wheelchair. Badshah was transferred to it. Mili and Ruhi decided the two of them would accompany him. Badshah was thrilled to have both of them with him. The ward boy pushed the wheelchair towards the lift. Mili and Ruhi kept pace with him.

The next morning everyone was in nail-biting tension. The biopsy report should come in today. What would it say? What was in the tumour? Was it malignant? Or was it benign? As the day wore on, they were told that the report will not be given now. The doctor would come in the evening and hand it over personally. A nurse came and gave them this information.

At this, Sanjay grew even more anxious. Was the report very bad? Was that why they were delaying it? Was that why the doctor wanted to hand it over personally? Mili too was in the throes of great anxiety. She could tell that something was not quite right about the report. She glanced at Sanjay. She glanced at Rintu. Both the faces looked tense. Bappa too had fallen silent. Ruhi and Rajveer were looking at one another and trying to gauge each other's thoughts. Sanjay left for the canteen upstairs. Ruhi followed, to give him company. Rintu and Bappa headed for the pathology department, where the report had most probably already come in. Mili and Rajveer stayed back with Badshah.

Sanjay asked for two cups of tea for Ruhi and for himself. Ruhi was aware that her father was under a lot of stress and he was trying to distract himself with some tea. She wanted to do the same as she said, 'I don't think there's anything seriously wrong with Bhai. The report cannot be too bad.' Sanjay said, 'Let us see. It doesn't look too good.' Ruhi said, 'Even if it is malignant there is treatment available. Don't worry. Bhai will be all right.'

In the meantime, Rintu and Bappa came into the canteen. Bappa narrated how Rintu had got into an argument with a doctor in the pathological department. Rintu had wanted to know why the biopsy report was not being shared with them even though it was ready. Dr Sudhir Desai said that Dr Raghuraman was busy in the OT. He will hand it over personally in the evening when he came for his rounds. He also wanted to have a discussion with them. Rintu did not want to accept this answer. His point was: how could the report be withheld from them just because the doctor was in the OT? If he wished to discuss things with them, he could do that later. But why would the biopsy report be held back?

After some back and forth of heated words, the two calmed down. It was decided that as soon as Dr Raghuraman came out of the OT, the report would be handed to them with his permission. With that Rintu and Bappa had to satisfy themselves and so they came to the canteen.

Everyone was grave, deep in thought. Each brow was wrinkled with worry and stress. They were afraid that there was indeed a malignancy report and that was the reason for the delay. The doctor wanted to hand it to them personally so that he could break the news gently, explain the course of treatment and answer their queries properly so that he could handle the situation if the relatives of the patient were too overcome with emotions.

Sanjay said, 'I feel we should finish our lunch.'

Ruhi said, 'We should eat quickly and go back to Bhai. Then Ma and Rajveer can come and finish their meal.'

They ordered food for everyone. Ruhi rushed through hers and went back to Badshah's cabin.

At about four in the evening a nurse informed them that Dr Raghuraman had asked for them in his chamber. Rintu, Bappa and Rajveer went to the doctor's chamber on the ground floor. He said, 'See, the report has come. It is not good. There is a malignancy, and it is a grade 4 tumour. This kind of tumours is notorious for repeated recurrence.'

Everyone was silent for a while. A little later Rintu asked, 'So now we have to start t he treatment for cancer?'

Dr Raghuraman replied, 'Certainly. You have a month's time. Within that time, you should decide where you will go for the treatment. But wherever you do it, both radiation and chemotherapy will have to be done.'

Bappa asked, 'Doctor, what is this type of tumour called?'

Dr Raghuraman said, 'Glioblastoma. I am very sorry to say that the survival rate for this kind of cancer is very low.'

With these words ringing in their ears, the three of them left the doctor's chamber. Now the question was, would they report the conversation in its entirety to Sanjay and Mili.

Rintu said, 'We can edit parts of it. They don't need to know all of it. We'll have to tell t hem that there is malignancy in the biopsy report and treatment has to be pursued.'

Rajveer said, 'I shall not tell Ruhi the whole thing either.'

All three of them proceeded towards the lift with their heads hanging low. There was a large crowd in front of the lift. They had no option but to wait.

6

DEADLY DISEASE

•••

This was a new chapter. The battle against cancer. The combat between life and death. This was not Badshah's fight alone. In this battle his Baba and Ma, his Didi and Dada, his Chhotka, his relatives, friends and everyone around him who had in some way participated in the long-drawn war against cancer, were all equal stakeholders. In the case of Badshah, it was not a small number. Of course, the number swelled over a period of time.

After returning from the hospital everyone sat down for a brainstorming session. In the course of the discussion, three choices emerged as possible treatment sites: Mumbai, Delhi and Bangalore. Rintu lived in Mumbai. The Tata Memorial Hospital or TMH was located in Mumbai. It was considered to be the best institution for treating cancer. It was devoted to the treatment of cancer alone, and patients came there from all parts of the country. It also treated visiting patients from neighbouring countries. There were other hospitals too.

Then came Delhi. Ruhi and Rajveer stayed in neighbouring Gurgaon. Bappa too lived there. Delhi had private hospitals like Apollo and Medanta, where treatment was expensive. That kind of cost was not a matter of joke. There were also a few government hospitals where the cost was a bit more manageable. Over and above all else, Delhi had AIIMS or the All India Institute of Medical Sciences. The cost of treatment was affordable there because it was a government hospital, and the standard of treatment was also very high. But there was one obstacle. AIIMS was very crowded. There was the crowd of regular people as well as the political leaders. In addition to all political leaders of every possible weightage, all the bureaucrats also went to AIIMS for treatment. Bureaucrats of the central government as well as of Delhi municipality, all levels of government servants sought treatment at AIIMS. Therefore, getting admission there was difficult. Even the Emergency there was always overflowing.

Then there was Bangalore. Columbia Asia did not have radiation machines. There were a few private hospitals and a few government hospitals. Kidwai Hospital specialized in cancer treatment. It was reputed as well as affordable.

But Bangalore was an unfamiliar city for all of them. Rintu or Bappa would not be able to stay here for long.

They would have to go back to their own stations. How long would Ruhi and Rajveer be able to stay away from their business? Would Sanjay be able to handle it all on his own? The following morning Bappa had to return to Delhi. Some urgent work had piled up in his office. He had taken a few days off and come rushing when he heard about Badshah. Everyone was depressed. No one had ever imagined that Badshah would suddenly be struck by this disease. His friends were also downcast. Nobody could accept the biopsy report for what it said. This was not just cancer, this was grade four. The most critical. Everyone had the same question on their minds and tongues: was there treatment available for this disease? Was it curable?

News had reached Badshah's office through Ritam. Once the gravity of the diagnosis was comprehended, every single member of the office, irrespective of age or designation, stood dumbfounded. How could this happen to Avik? The ever-smiling, amicable, peaceful, efficient young man was afflicted by such a disease! Such a wonderful person has a brain tumour, is malignant and grade four! No one could swallow this bitter pill. Everyone of his team members decided they would visit him the very next Sunday. Thereafter they would all put their minds to what else could be done for him.

Ritam brought the news to Sanjay that on Sunday, at around ten or eleven in the morning, all the people from the office would come to visit Avik.

In the meantime, Badshah's biopsy report was coming under the scanner amongst the family members—

sometimes Rintu–Rohan and Rajveer, and sometimes Ritam and Rupak were taking part in the discussions. Everyone was in two minds—was the report accurate? Could there be an error? Finally, it was decided that they would go for a second biopsy from another lab. The residents of Bangalore suggested NIMHANS: National Institute of Mental Health and Neuroscience. It was a reputed lab and their report should be foolproof. Besides, a second opinion was equally necessary before the further course of treatment was embarked upon.

With that decision made, Rintu, Rajveer and Rohan went to meet Dr Raghuraman. They said to him, 'We would all like to go for a second opinion. We want another biopsy done.' Dr Raghuraman was silent for a while. Then he said, 'Certainly, if all of you wish that, it can be done. But where?'

'NIMHANS,' Rintu replied.

Accordingly, Dr Raghuraman dispatched his instructions.

When the news reached the pathology department, Dr Sudhir Pai was furious. Sending the tumour sample to another lab? A direct challenge to his biopsy report?

Doctors usually have oversized egos. And if their diagnosis or their work is challenged, their anger knew no bounds. Often the outcome of this fury is not a pleasant sight.

Dr Sudhir Pai's displeasure did not take such an ugly turn, but he did give them a piece of his mind, 'Wherever you go, the report is not going to be any different. Yes, you must do this for your satisfaction—that's all.' Rintu and Co. did not respond to that.

The following day Rajveer had to leave for Delhi. Although his business was not large, it still needed supervision. He had been here in Bangalore from 3rd May to 11th May. Now he needed to return there. But no decision had been reached as yet, about Badshah's further treatment. Rajveer was in two minds. But Sanjay and Mili convinced him to go back. Ruhi was staying back.

Each day passed one by one, but the NIMHANS report showed no sign of emerging. Sanjay and Mili were hanging in balance, sometimes in hope and sometimes in the doldrums of anxiety. Could it be that the report was delayed because their findings differed from the Columbia Asia report? Perhaps the nature of the malignancy of the tumour was not quite so critical—perhaps it wasn't grade four. That would give them a lot of leeway. Dr Raghuraman had said that the disease would be far more treatable if it wasn't grade four. It could even open up a possibility of remission.

On the other hand, their worries also mounted with time. The delay could also indicate that their findings were far worse. Mili could recollect one afternoon as she ate lunch in the canteen, Dr Raghuraman had come in with a few other doctors in tow. He gazed at Mili fixedly and said something to the other doctors. They also turned to glance at Mili. Their eyes bore curiosity and pity—Mili was certain that it was Badshah's illness that had caused the pity to be there in their eyes.

If she were to connect that incident with the delay in the NIMHANS report, then the dark clouds of pessimism completely and utterly overshadowed any trace of hopes. Every time the gaze of those doctors that afternoon floated into Mili's mind, her heart sank with untold fears.

Sanjay wondered how, in a space of a few weeks, so much had happened in their lives, almost rendering it unrecognizable. How could Badshah contract this deadly disease? A hale and hearty youth who was working diligently, playing football in the weekends, having fun with friends his own age—how could he suddenly fall so sick? About ten days before the MRI was done in Columbia Asia on 2 May, Badshah's right limbs had started growing weak. He experienced difficulty walking and holding things with his right hand.

Sanjay remembered how he had called around 23-24 April and informed his father of this difficulty. He also mentioned that he had visited a doctor, who had prescribed medicines which he was having. Sanjay was a bit relieved at that. A few days later when they got to know that the medicines were not working, Sanjay and Mili both suggested changing the physician. Badshah too mentioned that with his friend's help, he was trying to schedule an appointment with a different doctor. He had gone with Ritam to Columbia Asia. And then all this happened.

Sanjay thought, about how quickly our lives can change. One may lose his job, one may have an accident, one may get critically ill, and one may die suddenly. In each case, the person concerned, and his or her family, were deeply affected. The trauma could be psychological, physical or financial. The extent of the damage seldom crossed the bounds of the family. This was a clear indication that family was at the center of human or social existence. The role of society, in the case of an individual's or a family's trauma, was merely to extend a helping hand in the form of financial or other help, condolences, and empathy. That was all. But the near and dear ones bore the entire brunt of that trauma. Why was this the case? Sanjay's understanding said to him that economics was the foundation of the social being's existence and the family was the fulcrum of the economy. The family walked hand in hand with economics and therefore the brunt of the trauma was borne by the family alone.

Ever since Badshah's diagnosis, Sanjay was unable to sleep well at night. He woke up at all odd hours. He was plagued by worries and fears. Sleep would elude him once he woke up. But staying awake brought a host of stranger thoughts and more unnamed fears. But he tried his best to keep his cool. This was no time to break down. There was too much to do, too much at stake.

At such a time, one Sunday morning, Badshah's office colleagues came to visit him—about twenty men and women in all. Badshah was delighted to see them. It was no small matter, getting so many of his colleagues in one place together. By that time Badshah was able to speak a little better, though not as well as normal. Everyone tried to boost his morale. They mentioned how all of them missed him. And they presented him with a large Get Well Soon card. Inside the card, there was a message that read:

The warmth of all our best wishes,

The abundance of our love and affection,

Will hasten you towards a speedy recovery.

You will get back your lively, energetic days,

Those bright and shining moments—we wish this for you!

Around this heartfelt message all of them had signed with short comments, which either harked back to an old memory for Badshah, or recollected an old quote of his, or reminisced some past moments of joy which would boost his morale for now.

Badshah was in no shape to read all the messages in detail. But the Get Well Soon card brought a smile to his lips and a teardrop in his eye. His expression indicated that he wanted to say a lot, but he was unable to. This inability cast a shadow of sorrow on his face, if only for a millisecond. His colleagues noticed this and they began to clap in unison, so that Badshah's mind would get distracted and he would forget his momentary sorrow. That is exactly what happened. The applause enthused Badshah so much that he extended his left hand towards them.

Ritam and another young lad their age grabbed his left hand to their hearts.

Sanjay, Mili and Ruhi witnessed the entire exchange. It remained in their minds as an example of how empowering the love and encouragement of empathetic peers can be for a patient suffering from a harsh disease such as Badshah's.

They stayed for almost two hours and finally, they left. Before leaving they tried to boost the morale of Sanjay and Mili as best they could. Then one of them, Amit Sachdeva, pulled Sanjay aside and took him to the lobby for a word in private. It was nearly one in the afternoon. Most visitors who had come for other patients had all left. The lobby was quite deserted. They pulled up a couple of chairs and Amit said to Sanjay, 'Uncle, in the office about a hundred of us have met and discussed Avik's case. All of us are very fond of Avik. We are very concerned about him and we all want him to get well soon. In that meeting, everyone contributed some cash to the extent of their abilities and gathered a fund. It comes to a lakh and thirty thousand rupees. I know this is a paltry sum. We are also trying to get the company to provide some financial assistance so that Avik gets the best of treatment. But that will take some time. Until then, you could use this nominal amount for his treatment. Please keep this.' Amit handed him a packet before he could say anything.

Holding the packet of cash in his hands, Sanjay looked Amit Sachdeva in the eye. He was not very old, perhaps in his early thirties. And yet so mature. Earlier Sanjay had spoken to him once when the biopsy report had come in with the diagnosis of the disease. Amit had wanted to know whether they had decided on the future course of action as far as treatment was concerned. He had asked about which hospital they were considering and an estimated cost of treatment there.

Sanjay had informed him then that it was undecided. But Mumbai looked like a strong possibility. For one, Rintu lived in Mumbai and that was a great advantage. Second, the best hospital in the country for the treatment of cancer was Tata Memorial and that was located in Mumbai. Amit had informed him that TMH did not offer the cashless privileges of Mediclaim insurance. But upon enquiry they also figured out that the cost of treatment at TMH was substantially lower than other private hospitals.

That day, in the course of their discussion they had calculated a ballpark figure of the cost involved in treating Badshah's cancer. It came to about eight to ten lakhs. Amit had promised to try his best to get the company to assist as much as possible. He had mentioned that all the employees of the office would have a meeting over this matter and take a decision on how they could be of more help to Avik.

This packet of cash which Amit handed to Sanjay a little while ago, was a result of that meeting. Some donated a day's salary. Some contributed five hundred or a thousand. Some pitched in with even greater amounts. All in all it came to a lakh and thirty thousand. Sanjay glanced at the packet. Badshah's face swam before his eyes.

He could not speak much. He thanked Amit and got up. He needed to inform Milli and Ruhi immediately. And yes, Badshah too. The only son of a retired bank employee was afflicted with a critical disease. His treatment required a lot of money. The boy's colleagues had come together and gathered a fund for his treatment, which was handed over by their representative to Avik's father today. When Sanjay reached Badshah's cabin, he found that all the office colleagues had already left. There were only Ruhi, Mili and Rohan in the room. Monica was also there, but she had gone downstairs to see the colleagues off. Monica too worked in the same company. She used to work in Infosys earlier. Later she joined the same company as Badshah. This could have been orchestrated by Badshah. They had been in a relationship for the past five years. They met at a tutorial class in Jamshedpur, got introduced and gradually developed feelings for one another. Monica had lost her mother when she was a child. She was raised by her grandmother.

When Badshah was told of the gesture his colleagues had made, his eyes glistened with unshed tears. In a soft voice he said, 'Baba, they love me.'

That was so true. Their love did not only translate to financial help. It showed through in myriad ways. Sanjay had witnessed it, as had others. Many people were moved by this. In this day and age, when people had grown so selfish and self-absorbed, such genuine affection for a colleague, and concern was rare indeed. His face bore the proof that he was very touched by it. He was also very happy at the thought that his parents were not just pleased by this show of love from his colleagues, rather they were moved. Badshah also knew that his father did not have a truckload of cash. He was worried, even in this state, about his long-drawn and expensive treatment. Sanjay was aware that Badshah was plagued by the thought that his medical insurance of four lakhs was nothing on the face of this kind of treatment. Therefore, he had informed Badshah about the larger aid package that was being worked out by the company, in addition to the personal hand of help that they had extended. This was so that he would stop worrying. It was important for him at this point in time.

Badshah was relatively relieved to hear all this. He sank back into his bed. His eyelids drifted shut and he tried to sleep. He still did not know that his biopsy report had diagnosed malignancy, or cancer. All he knew was that the burden of his treatment, which was going to weigh heavy on his father financially, had been partially lifted by t his gesture of his office colleagues. Over and above all the physical pain, Badshah was tormented by these worries incessantly.

7

ON THE WAY TO MUMBAI

...

Rintu had to return to Mumbai. There were some household responsibilities that required him to go back. He had wished to stay until Sunday so that he could meet Badshah's colleagues too. But instead, he had to leave one day earlier.

Meanwhile, the NIMHANS report did not show up even on Monday. Sanjay, Mili and Ruhi were discussing where they should take Badshah—Mumbai or Delhi, or should they stay back in Bangalore? All three of them agreed on one thing—the decision about further treatment will only depend on the quality of treatment and nothing else, not any of the inconveniences that the option may open up.

Mumbai would pose no problems for accommodation etc. since Rintu was there. As far as they had been able to gather information, TMH seemed to be the best option for cancer treatment. Still, Rajveer and Bappa were making their own enquiries in Delhi, about AIIMS, Medanta, Apollo and Rajeev Gandhi Cancer Hospital. In the case of Delhi the one question that they constantly came up against was: where would Badshah be put up? This was causing Delhi to slide down on the scale of choices.

Now Bangalore. Sanjay was not very clear about the treatment options in Bangalore, and how good they were. Mili and Ruhi were in the same boat. But Rohan and Monica did want that the subsequent treatment should happen in Bangalore, because they did not want to let him go out of their sight. They wanted to stay close to Badshah at this time. The relationships were different, but they both loved Badshah a lot. But they too were equally ignorant about the best options for treatment in Bangalore. Moreover, it would be impossible for Badshah to stay in his own flat because it was on the second floor and sans lift.

Therefore, it all boiled down to Mumbai. Yet, before they took the final decision, they decided to ask Badshah for his opinion as well. So, the question was posed to him. Ruhi asked him, 'Bhai, where do you think we should go next—Mumbai, Delhi or Bangalore?'

Badshah was silent for some time. Perhaps he was taking some time to mull over it. After such a momentous surgery on the brain, it was not easy to weigh options and come to a decision very quickly.

Ruhi continued, 'Bhai, you will need more treatment. Where do you think we should do it? Would you like Mumbai, or Delhi or Bangalore—tell us?'

Finally, Badshah spoke, 'Mumbai—with Chhotka. I shall go to Mumbai.' This choice of Badshah was not unexpected to Sanjay, Mili, or Ruhi. All of them were well aware of the deep trust Badshah reposed in his Chhotka. He felt instantly at ease at the very mention of Mumbai—because his Chhotka lived there.

Thereafter none of them had any doubts. Now it was time to book the tickets. Rohan was instructed to buy four air tickets using Badshah's laptop, for Sanjay, Ruhi, Mili, and Badshah. Bangalore to Mumbai. Before booking the tickets, Sanjay had a chat with Rintu, informing him of the difficulties with Delhi and Bangalore as options.

Rohan bought four air tickets on Badshah's laptop—Indigo Airlines, 18th May, at 12.30pm.

It was time to leave the hospital, but the report from NIMHANS still showed no signs of arriving. They began to call and plead from the morning of the 16th, but until the evening of the 17th there was no sign of it.

Everyone was busy speculating. They wondered if the result was very different from the findings of Columbia

Asia. Not just the family, even Rohan, Ritam and Monica were plagued by these worrisome questions.

Badshah was perhaps quite aware that he had a deep malady. The word cancer had not been uttered, but he knew that there was a tumour in his brain. In all likelihood, the possibility of cancer was plaguing him as well. Although he could not ask anyone directly, he would try to read their faces. Perhaps he could see through some of their hard-won acting skills. And Rohan, Ritam, and Monica could understand that. Alongside Badshah's treatment, and caring for him, these games of playacting and pretense were also running simultaneously in Badshah's cabin, in Columbia Asia.

Rohan and the others were waiting with bated breath for the report from NIMHANS—in the hope of a miracle. In the meantime, the date of their departure to Mumbai was nearly upon them. It was 17 May today. The flight was at 12.30 pm the following day. Rohan said to Sanjay, 'Uncle, let us go and speak to the doctors about the biopsy report. There's no more time. You must leave tomorrow and Avik has to be discharged before that.'

At this, Sanjay, Ruhi and Rohan proceeded to the pathology department on the second floor. They were told that the report had not yet come in. And more important, the sample that was sent for biopsy, or the 'block', had also not come back to Columbia Asia.

This was a matter of grave concern. Without the 'block' there was no point in going to Mumbai. No hospital there would start the treatment without the 'block'. They would first conduct their biopsy with the 'block' and based on that, they would start the treatment. Sanjay asked a nurse there, 'Where does the manager sit?'

The nurse replied, 'On the ground floor.'

Sanjay, Ruhi, Rohan, and Ritam trooped into the manager's office. Mili and Monica stayed with Badshah. The manager was in his chamber. Sanjay broached the topic, 'We need the "block" and the report both by the end of the day. Tomorrow our flight is at 12.30 pm. We must leave the hospital at 10 am.'

The manager said, 'Let me have a look into the matter. Please have a seat.'

He left the room and headed for the lift. Sanjay and Co. were right behind him. He reached the pathology department on the second floor. Before going in, the manager said to them, 'Please wait here, outside. I'll find out about this and be right back.'

Ten minutes later the manager came back with his update. The gist of it was: the 'block' had been sent to NIMHANS as per Sanjay and the family's wishes. So far neither the 'block' nor the report has come in. Since NIMHANS was a reputed research institute, it was notoriously busy. Perhaps that was the reason for the delay.

Now Ritam spoke up, 'It is almost a week now, and yet the report hasn't come in. And there have been no initiatives from you all over here?'

Rohan added, 'Sir, are you aware that the patient is leaving for Mumbai tomorrow? The next set of investigations and treatments will happen over there. But we need the "block" and the report before we leave. Especially the "block". Without that, the treatment cannot begin.'

Now the manager seemed to wake up from his stupor. He instantly asked a staff of the pathology department to call up NIMHANS and ask them to send the 'block' and the report to Columbia Asia that very day. The staff member started speaking to someone in NIMHANS, trying to explain the urgency of the matter to him. A little later he held the phone away from his ears and said, 'Sir, it is almost 6 pm now. Today nothing more is possible. But they have promised to send it tomorrow by 10-10.30 am.'

Sanjay said, 'We will be out of here by 10 am. How do we get it in hand before that?'

The manager spoke to the staff member and he in turn spoke to the employee at NIMHANS. They conferred amongst themselves softly. Finally, the manager came up to Sanjay and said, 'Please go ahead with your plans of leaving for Mumbai tomorrow. You will leave from here at 10 am, right? You'll get the "block" and the report in your hands before you leave.'

This left no room for further conversation. Ritam said, 'Come on Uncle, let us clear the hospital bill. We should finish it tonight so that nothing is left for tomorrow.'

Rohan too agreed, 'Yes, let us get that out of the way, Uncle.'

Sanjay and Ritam went up to the TPA counter on their floor. TPA stood for Third Party Administrator.

A young man of about thirty sat at the desk. When Ritam gave the patient's name, he located Badshah's details on the computer and scanned it. Then he said, 'Until tonight your bill comes to four lakhs and thirty-one thousand. Since you are discharging the patient tomorrow morning, there will be no charges for tomorrow. Twelve noon is the checkout time.'

Ritam said, 'Yes, well, we shall leave by 10 am. Our flight is at 12.30 pm.'

The young man said, 'All right then, I shall make the final bill and email it to the insurance company so that they can settle it by tonight. You will face no difficulties tomorrow. Just give me a few minutes.'

'Fine then. We shall be back after half an hour,' Ritam said. Then he asked, 'Can we make the payment by credit card or must we pay in cash?'

'Both are fine. You can even make part payment in cash and the rest by credit card.'

Sanjay and Ritam were relieved as they left. Sanjay felt they should go back to Badshah now. He hadn't seen his son's face in a long time. In the cabin he found Badshah chatting with Mili and Monica. She was talking about their office—who said what when they heard about Badshah's illness, who came for the meeting they had about him and what was discussed in that meeting, etc. Badshah was naturally curious about all of it. He wanted to know more about those people who had not come to visit him, but had attended the meeting held for him in office. He wished to know whether they were fully updated about his illness or not, whether they had contributed to the common fund, if there were any significant reasons behind their inability to visit him at the hospital etc. He was full of hundred such questions, because he was aware that the meeting held for him at work was a large one. It had been summoned at a time when workers of both shifts could attend it. The arrangements were all made by the manager, Amit Sachdeva. Nearly a hundred employees had attended that meeting. Amit had briefed everyone at the start of the meeting, about Badshah's condition. Many well-wishers like Soumya had suggested pooling their resources into a common fund. In this Ritam and Monica had also played a role. A few of the senior management were also present at the meeting. Everyone had agreed wholeheartedly to pitching in for Avik. Actually Badshah, aka Avik, was very well liked and accepted by everyone because of his work and his behaviour. All those who knew him, thought well of him. He was in the hospital for quite a few days now. And even before that he had been unable to go to work for a few days. He thought of his office, his colleagues, every now and then. Especially when he gained a bit of respite from his physical symptoms or when no one was present in his cabin, except perhaps people like Monica or Mili. In those moments such thoughts drifted into his mind often. Today too, he wanted to know all this because Monica was at hand. She herself had not been present at the meeting, but she was updated with every detail of it and she was describing it all to him. He was listening intently. Sometimes a ripple of delight passed over his face, sometimes a few questions bubbled into his mind and a few times shades of worry or concern cast their shadow on his face.

Mili was also listening to these stories eagerly. She enjoyed hearing about his popularity. She had always believed that her son was shy, introverted, and could not talk to people easily. But that idea that had grown over many years bore no resemblance to all that she had witnessed, all that she had heard after coming to Bangalore. This was like a new discovery. After his illness, Mili felt she was discovering a whole new Badshah altogether.

Sanjay said to Badshah, 'Son, we leave tomorrow from here at around ten. The flight is at half past twelve. You are mentally prepared, right?'

'Yes Baba, I am ready. Who all are going?'

'You, Didi, Ma and I. Chhotka is already there.'

Badshah's eyes brightened with joy.

Suddenly Ritam burst into the room and said, 'Uncle, come, the bill is ready. Let's get that out of the way.'

Sanjay nodded and left the cabin hastily with Ritam.

The total bill came to four lakhs, thirty thousand, five hundred and fifty-eight rupees. Of which the insurance would reimburse three lakhs, seventy-two thousand, three hundred and twenty rupees. The rest would be borne by Sanjay. The amount came to fifty-eight thousand, two hundred and thirty-eight rupees. Sanjay could have used the debit card to pay. But then he remembered that the cash that was contributed by Badshah's colleagues, which Amit Sachdeva had handed over to Sanjay, was lying there. That was a sum of one lakh and thirty thousand rupees. So, he decided to use that to make the payment.

Sanjay picked up the phone and called Mili. The cash was with her. She came over to the billing counter and counted out the amount to Sanjay. The young man at the counter counted the money once again and handed a receipt to Sanjay instantly. They went back to Badshah's cabin. It was nearly seven in the evening. They must head back to Badshah's flat now. Ritam too started to pack up his things and head home. They must be back here early the next day. Although the billing formalities were done, there were a few other protocols such as collecting the discharge certificate and also the fit-to-fly certificate for Badshah. Without that they would not allow him to board the flight. Rajveer had alerted them to this. His father who used to work in Spicejet, had prompted him to give this reminder in time.

Sanjay, Mili and Ruhi would have to pack up all their things and leave Badshah's flat early the next day. Then they would have to reach the hospital, get Badshah ready, complete all the documentation, collect certificates—there was a lot to do.

Sanjay reminded Ritam to get there early the next day.

Rohan would stay the night with Badshah. Rohan had not left his side for even a single night and the final night in Columbia Asia too, he wanted to spend with Badshah. Who knew when they would see each other again.

The next day, as soon as Monica and Ruhi reached Badshah's cabin, they started packing up his things. Sanjay went in search of the Sister to get the discharge certificate. The paperwork was all ready. Sanjay just needed to sign in a few places. Then there was the fit-to-fly certificate. The Sister said, 'Dr Raghuraman will be here soon. He will make it as soon as he comes.'

Sanjay came back to the cabin with the paperwork. By then a lot of the work was done. Ritam too had arrived.

Badshah was a bit excited, and a bit sad as well. He would get to leave the hospital after many days, and on the other hand he would have to say goodbye to Monica and Rohan.

Badshah was wondering, 'Will they be able to come and see me in Mumbai? Will I see them anytime soon?' His mind was quite in a turmoil.

Meanwhile the Sister began to explain Badshah's medication schedule to Mili. They were just two in number, but t hey needed to be given regularly at a set time. The Sister informed Sanjay that Dr Raghuraman had arrived. He could pick up the fit-to-fly certificate in a short while. Before leaving, the Sister hugged Badshah and stroked his cheeks as she said, 'You will get well soon. Never lose hope. Just follow what the doctors are saying. We wish you the very best.'

Badshah nodded. There was concurrence with the Sister's advice in his nod, and there was gratitude for the affection shown by the Sister, and for her best wishes.

Sanjay was just heading for the office to collect the fit-to-fly certificate when suddenly Dr Raghuraman rushed in with a piece of paper in his hand.

'Good Morning!' Sanjay said.

'Good Morning!' The doctor replied, 'Here is the fit-to-fly certificate.' Then he walked up to Avik and said, 'Good Morning! How are you Avik?'

Avik replied, 'Fine.'

Then the doctor asked Sanjay, 'What time are you leaving?'

'Ten o'clock,' Sanjay replied.

'All right. I am hoping the report and the "block" from NIMHANS will be here before that. In case it doesn't, we shall arrange to send it to the airport.'

Ritam spoke up, 'Sir, Rohan and I shall stay back. We can take the report and the "block" to the airport.'

The doctor said, 'That is also a possibility. Let me see what I can do.' He then wished Avik all the very best, and left.

Now they began to get ready to leave. Badshah was made to dress in his normal clothes, T-shirt, and jeans.

Monica put his shoes on for him. Ruhi had packed his odds and ends into a small bag. Rohan booked a cab on the app. It would arrive in about ten minutes.

At this time the Sister arrived with a few junior nurses. They had all come to wish Avik good luck. A ward boy had also arrived with a wheelchair.

It was time to leave Columbia Asia. Badshah was a trifle emotional. He had spent fifteen momentous days there. He had come in here on 2 May, with Ritam and Monica. They consulted Dr Guruswamy. Then there was the MRI and based on that report the admission into the hospital. Ritam called Sanjay. On 4 May Ma, Baba, Didi, Dada, Chhotka, everyone reached Bangalore. Badshah remembered it all clearly.

Then the surgery on 5 May. The evening before the surgery, his colleagues had come to the hospital to boost his morale. Badshah was so touched by the fact that there were at least twenty-five to thirty people running after his stretcher as he was wheeled into the OT, and just before the doors shut, they had screamed 'Best of Luck' in one voice!

As he was leaving the hospital the memories were flooding back. He remembered how the nurses would gather around him during physiotherapy sessions, rooting for him and egging him on—it had really moved him. Once he even sang a song for all of them. At first, he was humming and when they requested, he sang it out loud: *bade ache lagtey hain, yeh nadiyan, yeh dharti* …Badshah sang the entire song and the four or five nurses listened in silence. Sanjay and Mili were also there. They had found everyone to be very affectionate in the hospital, almost like family. Today, as he was leaving, going far away from all of them, Badshah felt quite despondent.

There were other reasons too. Leaving Bangalore would mean not seeing Monica every day. He would also lose touch with Rohan and Ritam. Would they be able to come to Mumbai? Before the disease, his life had been different. It was chockful of joy and excitement, with his office, friends, his football matches. The weeks would fly without his knowing. In the weekends the football matches kept him busy. There were so many friends there too. Badshah was the center of attention there too. The company also had a football team and the inter-office football matches were held in Bangalore. Their team always participated. In 2014 they were the runners-up. Now he was having to leave everything behind. Naturally, the heart was heavy.

Ritam said the cab was waiting downstairs. They would have to go down now. The ward boy helped Badshah into the wheelchair and began to wheel him towards the lift. Rohan and Ritam had picked up the suitcases that belonged to Sanjay and Mili. Ruhi carried her own bag. Monica placed a hand on Badshah's wheelchair as she matched her steps with it. Sanjay and Mili walked beside her.

The cab was waiting at the main entrance of the hospital. Mili, Ruhi and Badshah sat in the rear and Sanjay sat in front, beside the driver.

When they reached the Bangalore airport, they checked in their luggage, picked up the boarding passes and went and sat in the waiting lounge. Rohan and Ritam would soon be here with the report and the 'block'. These had not arrived from NIMHANS at the t ime that the group left Columbia Asia. They had decided that Rohan and Ritam would come to the airport with it. They arrived nearly half an hour later—Rohan, Ritam and Monica. Sanjay had kept his eyes peeled. When they were at the entrance gate, he walked up to them because they would not be allowed inside the airport. Ritam held the 'block' and the report in his hands. Sanjay took it from him. Then they brought Badshah's wheelchair to the entrance. They were on the other side of the gate and Badshah was on the inside. They were quite worked up.

Rohan said, 'Keep your spirits strong—all will be well.'

Ritam said, 'Avik, you're a fighter—you'll win for sure!'

Monica did not say anything. She just raised her right hand and waved. Badshah was silent too. His head was shaven due to the surgery. He wore a cap on it. Slowly, he raised his left hand. His eyes were deep pools of calm. In the throes of a nightmare, they bore a strong ray of hope.

Suddenly the loudspeaker boomed: passengers for Mumbai were being asked to proceed for security check.

Ruhi came and alerted them, 'Baba, we must go now.'

Badshah waved goodbye to them. They returned his wave.

Sanjay turned the wheelchair in the opposite direction and began to wheel it away slowly towards the security check area. Halfway there, he turned back. The three friends still stood there, gazing fixedly at Sanjay and Badshah.

8

NEW CITY

•••

Patna may not be a metropolis, but it was not a small city either. From east to west, or from Patna city to Danapur, it was twenty kilometers in length. In breadth it was less—about five kilometers. The population density was comparatively high. Especially since the two banks of the Ganga were joined by the mammoth bridge, the population of Patna had increased considerably. In the north of Bihar, agriculture was the primary livelihood source. A handful of cities and towns provided some industrial scope. But it was all Patna-centric. The rest of the state was entirely dominated by agriculture. Despite the presence of prominent rivers, irrigation systems were not efficiently laid out and on top of that there was the pestilence of floods. Almost every year there were floods. Therefore, living conditions were deplorable for the people of northern Bihar.

Ever since the bridge was built over the Ganga, many working-class people had migrated to Patna. Some worked as labourers, some as coolies, others pushed carts and most of them were rickshaw pullers. Although Patna was home to palatial bungalows, luxurious shops, showrooms and malls, the rickshaws were still the primary mode of transportation. If one did now own one's own set of wheels, willy-nilly the rickshaw was your only choice. Hence, thousands of rickshaws could be seen plying the streets of the city. The landless labouring class, when pushed to the edge, would emigrate to Patna—they would be able to eke out a living by either helping build mansions, or carry heavy cargo from here to there, or work behind a sales counter of a shop for meager wages or at least, push a cart or pull a rickshaw. The population explosion in Patna was therefore, inevitable.

Patna was not a city, in that sense. Some areas were quite crowded, stuffy and dingy. But the weather was quite temperate and enjoyable. Summers and winters were a bit extreme, but if one could adjust to that, it was a pleasant place to be in. It was not humid and sticky like Kolkata and the water in Patna was quite good.

All in all, Sanjay liked Patna. It was twenty-five years since he had quit Patna and settled in Jamshedpur. But still, he could not forget Patna. At the drop of a hat, he would compare the two cities, and place Patna above Jamshedpur.

But why this adulation? Why this affection? In truth, from a very young age, all the way through his teenage and youth, Sanjay had lived in Patna. His education, his football, first love, firm friendships, political awakening, and the beginning of his career were all enacted on the grounds of Patna city. In short, the man that Sanjay was, had been crafted almost in its entirety in Patna's workshop. That is a fact!

Sanjay came to Patna at the age of eleven. In those days Patna was considerably greener and emptier. Sanjay's Kaka (uncle) was in Sales in Usha Co. He would often visit Patna. There would be exhibitions of the Usha Co. products—such as sewing machines, ceiling fans, table fans etc.—at Patna's Gandhi Maidan or elsewhere. Kaka or Sujit Roy was a familiar name in the regional sector of Usha Co. Whenever he visited Patna, he would stay at a hotel in Ashok Marg. It was called Oasis Hotel, right opposite BN College. He had a colleague called Srivastava, who hailed from Uttar Pradesh. Sanjay used to call him Srivastava Uncle. He did not know his first name. He too would tour the entire region of Bihar with Sanjay's uncle, obviously with Patna as the center of their activities. Both the men would patronize the Oasis Hotel when they were in Patna. Once they arrived in the city and went into the hotel, only to hear that the hotel was up for sale. The owner—Mr. Singh—was selling the hotel and moving back to his hometown, Hajipur, which was to the north of Patna, across the river.

At the time there was no bridge over the Ganga and crossing the river was a momentous matter. There were a few steamers that did the job. The handful of steamers were owned by a powerful zamindar called Baccha Babu. He was known far and wide. The owner of Hotel Oasis was related to Baccha Babu. Kaka and Srivastava-ji bought the hotel from him. But the owner of the premises remained the same since Kaka and Srivastava-ji were short of funds and so they could not buy the entire property. Hence, the hotel came under the ownership of the three of them as equal shareholders.

Even a one-third share in a flourishing business such as Hotel Oasis was not a small matter for Sanjay and his family. In Kolkata, Sanjay's father did not have a job. As a skilled footballer, he had managed to acquire jobs, but he could never hold on to one. No one ever understood why he was so callous, despite being a reputed player. For this reason, Sanjay's mother was always in the depths of misery. Tears were her constant companions. Although he was the younger of the two brothers, Kaka's contribution to their family was something that Sanjay, Partha and Rintu would never forget. In his commitment to give his mother, his Dada-Boudi and his three nephews a decent life, Kaka never did get around to marrying, although love had brushed his life and knocked on his door two times. Once in his early youth and once in his greying years. Both the times he had turned it away for the sake of the greater family.

It was Kaka who, in his eagerness to give his Dada a decent source of livelihood and to save Sanjay and his brothers from the daily strife of poverty, bought the Hotel Oasis in Patna with the intent of shifting the entire family to Patna. Since Sanjay's father was unemployed at the time, struggling to feed his sons let alone educate them, he had no objections to shifting to Patna, lock stock and barrel. In fact, he felt it was a golden opportunity, a fresh chance, and it thrilled him. At first Sanjay's mother and his grandmother were hard pressed to accept the departure from Kolkata for good. Especially for the people who were born, raised and grown in Kolkata, it was a tough prospect indeed. It was heart-rending to think of leaving behind familiar faces, friends, relatives, known alleyways, every street and its corners and even the pond by the house and the weirdly shaped flora around it. It felt like shedding a skin and entering a whole new body, while the mind, the memories still remained intact.

Sanjay's grandmother was a strongminded woman. She could stand tall in the face of the greatest adversities. She had lost her husband early. But she did not lose heart. She recovered her spirits and held firm the helm of her household. In a household of meagre means, she had handled many a crisis singlehandedly. On the face of mighty storms, she had shielded her daughter-in-law, encouraged her grandchildren. But there was just one weak spot where grandmother was powerless—her blind adulation of her sons. At times it did make her partial and unjust. She could hear no ill of her sons. Her elder son, when he failed to hold down a single job, and spent his days in the company of his friends, was still—in her eyes—above reproach. It is true that Bapi Roy was a renowned footballer in the football clubs of Kolkata. Those were the heydays of Kolkata football. On the one hand for East Bengal there were the famous five Pandavas or Sahlay, Venkatesh, Dhanraj, Apparao and Ahmed and on the other hand Mohan Bagan boasted players like Badru Banerjee and Sunil Sen. At such a time, playing for a club like Arian was not a matter of joke. It was not only football that he excelled in. Sanjay's father was also a talented singer and later in life, he made a name for himself on the stage as well. And about this elder son—Bapi Roy—and his irresponsibility, no one had ever heard grandmother utter a single word. On the contrary, if anyone ever brought it up, grandmother would sulk so hard that the topic would have to be changed. Grandmother was completely blind to Sanjay's father's faults.

Sanjay and his brothers called grandmother 'Thamma' and her younger son Kaku. Kaku was always ailing as a child, with an asthmatic constitution and later a victim of piles. These two ailments kept Kaku always under the weather. Especially as he grew older. But of course, in 1964 Kaku was still quite young and capable of taking on a lot. And that is why he was able to take a momentous decision such as moving the family, lock stock and barrel, from Kolkata to Patna.

Although everyone came around, Sanjay's mother was quite unwilling to go along with the decision. Even the thought of leaving Kolkata for good made her very sad indeed. The three sons of course did not care much either way. The youngest of them all was really too small. He was barely five years old, incapable of much thought. The two older ones were able to think and conceive a few things. They knew that their life in Kolkata was a harsh one—sometimes not enough food, sometimes the landlord hassling them for unpaid rent, and sometimes struggling to get the school authorities to allow them to take their exams, having paid only half the fees.

The thought flashed in their heads that perhaps a move to Patna would provide release from this condition. Perhaps they would gain a peaceful and hassle-free life. For them it meant a lot. If the possibilities that they were hearing about this move to Patna were actually true, if they could gain a halfway decent living, if the sons could be given a better education—these were eventually the thoughts that made their mother finally capitulate.

On 1 January 1964, Kaku boarded the Janat Express from Howrah to Patna, with the entire family in tow. Their father had already reached Patna and he was waiting to receive them at the station. The Roy family stepped into a new world that was culturally and linguistically totally different from their original world. There were geographical differences too. Kolkata had a more temperate weather, safe from extremes of either winter or summer. Patna was prone to extreme weather at both ends of the year. Food habits of the two cities was different. Patna was not as much of a fish-loving city as Kolkata was. These days the availability of fish has increased, but it was different then.

The family landed up in a two-roomed house in Rajendranagar. It was reasonably clean. The seven of them were a bit of a squeeze in the two rooms. One toilet made it that much more difficult. Yet, it was far better than the one and a half rooms of Kolkata, with its common toilet shared with other families. The house in Patna had a strip of a garden that was an instant mood-lifter. The garden had jasmine, hibiscus and also a few rose bushes. As they left for school every morning, the children had an eyeful of the flowers in the garden.

Sanjay, Partha and Rintu were admitted into Ram Mohan Roy Public School. Sanjay was in class six, Partha in class five and Rintu in class one. It was a Hindi medium school. That was tough on all three children. Everything was new for them—new school, new milieu, new language.

But soon after getting admitted into the school, they had to shift house. Probably something to do with rent again. The children were kept in the dark about the matter. All they knew was that there was some bitterness and they moved to Road number 10.

In the meantime, something else happened quite silently. Mr Srivastava, who owned one third of the Hotel Oasis, sold his share to the owner of the premises and went away to Kanpur. So now, Kaku was left with only one-third share in the business, while the landlord held two-thirds. This information reached the house a little while later. Mother and grandmother grew sombre. The outcome of this handover was known to Kaku and Baba, and even the women of the family could gauge which way the water will flow. One day Rintu asked to go to Oasis. They had gone there at least thrice by then. Each time they had sat in a cabin, feeling self-important and thrilled. Sanjay remembered eating in a restaurant in Kolkata during Durga Puja once. That was the first time he had tasted the pleasure of eating outside, in a formal restaurant. In Oasis they got back that same pleasure. It wasn't as posh as that restaurant in Kolkata, but Oasis had a standard of its own. They would order food and it would be brought to the cabin. The three children would roam here and there and after some fun and games, they would come back home.

But this time when Rintu asked to go to Oasis, Mother said no. Sanjay had already overheard his grandmother say that they were no longer equal partners in the hotel. So he explained to the younger ones that Father and Kaku no longer had the same hold over Oasis. They were now the minor partner and one Mr Singh or Singh Uncle was the major partner. He was the big guy now. God knows how much Rintu had comprehended at the age of five, but he had fallen silent. Never again did he ask to visit Oasis.

In a month or so the final call came. Mr Singh asked Kaku and Father to sell him their share for a nominal sum, so that he could gain full control over the business. The hotel was doing quite well and he did not want to split the profits. It was easy to bring pressure to bear upon a helpless duo of brothers from Kolkata who had no money, no influence and a family to care for.

Kakau and Father did protest a bit. But the opposition was stronger. They were forced to relinquish their share in the business for a nominal sum of money. So the two brothers were once again without a job. The only difference was that this time they had a little money in hand. But this was not the old familiar Kolkata. It was an unknown quantity, it was a new state called Bihar. Although it was the neighbouring state of West Bengal, the language spoken here was Hindi. In Kolkata Hindi was spoken fairly well, having many refugees from different neighbouring states. But it was not proper Hindi. It carried Bengali accents and was peppered with words shared by both Bengali and Hindi. Having a nodding acquaintance with that kind of Hindi still did not lend Father and Kaku the wherewithal to assimilate into the workforce of Patna city. They had no job, no business, no familiarity with the city and nobody to lean on for temporary relief and support. All they had was a few thousand rupees which would barely last a year for the entire family. There were three growing children in the house. They needed to be raised and educated—it was a huge challenge. Sanjay's grandmother grew a spine of steel on the face of this calamity. Sanjay's mother was heartbroken. The dreams that she had nurtured for a short while, on the strength of which she had bid adieu to her own parents, her extended family and come to a strange city leaving her homeland behind, seemed to shatter on the face of a cruel storm. But Mother also realized that she could not afford to grow weak. The circumstances were hostile. She needed to fight with her fist clenched and her teeth gritted.

The three brothers also understood the gravity of the situation. Barring Rintu who was too young to feel much, Sanjay and Partha could comprehend the seriousness of the situation in varying degrees. Many questions swirled in their heads—like why did Father and Kaku have to give up their share in the hotel which was doing so well? Why did they have to sell it to Singh Uncle?—but who would answer their questions?

Every morning Father and Kaku would leave the house in search of a job or an occupation, even a small business idea. Something that would require a small capital and more work. Kaku must have been barely thirty years old. He was always inclined towards a job. Father was about three years older. But he had never had the propensity to work at a job.

Amidst this turbulent turmoil, the household began to run on the capital they had received from the sale of the business. Sanjay and his brothers' education was uninterrupted, although the path was not a smooth one. In a short while the payment of fees began to get irregular. Before every annual examination they would be informed that the fees needed to be paid in full before they could appear for the exams. Perforce, there would be some scrounging around and somehow the amount would be raised. Fees would be paid and the children would take their exams. This train of events haunted them until they graduated from school. Every time they would prepare for exams and their hearts would quake in fear—would they actually get to take the exams? Or would they have to come back from the exam hall without being allowed to sit for it?

Their education had muddled along in this fashion. It left an impact on their results, naturally. They could have performed better, in different circumstances. But none of them had ever failed.

The three of them suffered from a complex because of their inability to pay the school fees on time. There was a date fixed for the fees to be submitted by, every month. That day there would be no studies. The class teacher would come into the class and each student would walk up to the desk and pay the fees. When everyone had paid the fees, they would be let off for the day. For that reason, on that day, students were exempted from wearing the school uniform.

On one such day Sanjay had gone to school wearing regular clothes, not to pay the fees, but to meet friends and hang out with them. Sanjay's youngest aunt had sent material for clothes to be stitched for Durga Puja. For this occasion all their relatives usually sent something or the other—either cash or material for clothes. With the cloth sent by the youngest aunt, the three brothers received shirts stitched to their sizes. Sanjay wore that shirt to school that day. When Sanjay reached the classroom, the class-teacher—Nilangshu babu—was collecting the fees. He saw Sanjay and immediately asked, 'Have you brought the fees?'

The question threw Sanjay for a second. He never paid the fees on the specified date and today was no exception. He stammered a bit and replied, 'No Sir, I haven't.'

That did it! The teacher went up in flames. He raised his voice and said, 'So then, why exactly have you deigned to put in an appearance? To show off your new shirt?' Even before Sanjay could reply, he hollered, 'Come here!'

Now Sanjay was certain that there was going to be a beating. Yet he dragged his feet and went up to his fuming class-teacher. Instantly he was rewarded with a tight slap on his left cheek, along with a roar, 'Showing off, eh!'

Sanjay knew that there was no space for a comeback. It was clear that Nilangshu Babu was not looking for a reply. Perhaps he had acted on the spur of the moment, in the throes of anger. But was this anger directed at Sanjay? He was not really at fault, except for wearing a new shirt that day. Perhaps there was another reason for his anger and it came out on Sanjay!

Much later, after careful consideration, Sanjay had come to the conclusion that many kinds of disequilibrium were embedded in the fabric of society. They manifested themselves through different relationships, which moved in cycles, in their familiar orbits. And this cyclical movement gave birth to conflicts.

This incident left a deep impact on Sanjay's mind. He got a firsthand experience of poverty in all its complex glory. The varied manifestations of poverty and its subtle powerplay revealed itself to him in its entirety. He would have never known or imagined until then that wearing a new shirt to school could turn into such a huge issue. After much deliberation on the incident, Sanjay had summarized it thus for himself: his crime was that he did not pay the school's fees on time, but he had instead dared to appear on that specified date wearing a new shirt.

Sanjay had many more opportunities in the years to come, to be humiliated on account of poverty. But that first incident had left the deepest mark on his mind. The impoverished, needy faces of all those around him had revealed themselves to his eyes in the starkest form that day. His intellect had grown restless to seek answers to why life was so ugly and unsavoury. He grew more alert and sensitive to his surroundings. His heart bled watching the traumatic and hungry form of poverty. He began to ponder on the nature of poverty, at length. Sometimes he felt the unrelenting nature of poverty was an absolute truth, it could not be touched. There was no release from it.

Sanjay cleared his Matric, or tenth grade, with decent marks in the second division. He wished to take up Science in college. He submitted his form accordingly in Patna's BN College. But he did not get the interview call because the cut off marks were even higher. His mother had wanted him to study Science. But all his efforts were in vain. He missed the opportunity for ten marks.

Eventually he had to change the stream and opt for Commerce. He relinquished the hope of studying Science and took admission in Patna College for Commerce. In those days it was a stream that was greatly in fashion. In 1969 banks were nationalized. Almost every day a new branch or some bank would open up. The demand for skilled professionals was growing and would grow further in the years to come. Everyone close to him said Commerce is a good choice, jobs would be easy to come by. Sanjay's mother was a bit sad at first. But on the advice of everyone, and with the hopes of a good job becoming easier, she consoled herself. A job was greatly needed and everyone knew how much the household would benefit when the eldest son got a job.

Sanjay began to go to college and attend classes. But he was not happy. All his classmates were from well-to-do households. They hung out in smaller, discrete groups. They came in to class together, spent their time together and left together. They never spared Sanjay a second glance. And neither did he try to interact with them. Their ways were totally different. Their faces bore the stamp of pride and arrogance. Some of them came to college in cars driven by chauffeurs who dropped them off and then picked them up. The rest came in scooters or bikes. Very few came in rickshaws.

Sanjay usually commuted on foot. The college was not too far from his home. By then his family had left Rajendra Nagar and moved to Chaitolla. It was even closer to the colleges. After a few months passing in this fashion, suddenly one day he found Satyajit in class. Satyajit had studied in the same school as Sanjay, in Raja Ram Mohan

Roy Seminary. Although they were in the same class, the sections were different. They may not have been bosom friends, but they were familiar with each other. Finding Satyajit here seemed like a boon for Sanjay. At least now he could sit with someone in class, discuss the course and generally hang out with.

The house in Chaitolla into which Sanjay's family had moved, or rather had been forced to move, was a small, independent house. Although it had three rooms, it really had no grace or style. One room was fairly large, but the other two rooms were barely big enough. One of them was eight feet by five feet—the size of a store-room or a puja room. The other one had an asbestos roof and measured about ten feet by seven feet. That room was occupied by Sanjay's grandmother and Kaku. One had to cross an open corridor to reach that room. On one side of that corridor was a tiny kitchen. Summers were all right, but monsoons and winters were difficult. Sanjay, his siblings and his parents occupied the large room. The store room in the middle was not put too much use. It contained a clothes rack and was used as wardrobe and dressing room by everyone. When Sanjay was a little older, he used to sleep in that room. That took some load off the large room. There was only one toilet, and that wasn't much to speak of.

The landlords were Bengalis—three brothers in all. The eldest was Nandakumar Palit and he lived in a large house nearby with his mother. The other two brothers lived in different cities. Sanjay and his family lived in that house for sixteen years. So many events, so many people, comings and goings, such incidents, so much joy and sorrows that house was a witness to. For three years they were unable to pay the rent so the landlords cut the electric connection. Water was short to begin with. But in those three years they were deprived of water in the one tap that they were privy to, as a reprisal for defaulting on the rent. They had struggled through that difficult time, without electricity and water.

But to this day, Sanjay has kept the memories of that house, the time in it, alive with great care. He still feels a lot of emotion when he remembers those days. The best days of his life can be found in those years, when Sanjay had received a divine touch of love despite and through the poisonous bites of poverty. He had received, in those years, a bunch of friends who were not just good human beings, but who loved the human race, society, the country and entire planet. It is not that Sanjay found those friends within that house. But the years that he spent in that house had given him a lot. Sanjay and his family had come in contact with many families, many neighbours during those years, who had turned the roughshod desert of poverty into a calming, cool oasis of faith in human nature. These people had reinstated his faith in the basic goodness of man, helping him to fight his way out of the cornered state that his financial condition had placed him in.

In these hard, strife-ridden times Sanjay had met Bimal-da while playing in the field next door. He still remembers the first question posed to him by Bimal-da, 'Do you play only cricket or football too?'

Sanjay and a few other boys his age played cricket in the small field adjacent to the house. Whether they had classes in college or not, whether they attended those classes or not, Sanjay and a few other boys were sure to play cricket in the field in the evenings. Partha and Rintu were also a part of this group. Actually, sport was a great magnet in Sanjay's family. His father and his Kaka had both played seriously in Kolkata. Baba had mostly played football and Kaka cricket. Sanjay preferred football to cricket. Hence he had answered Bimal-da with, 'I play both, but I prefer football.'

Bimal-da said, 'Very good. I too prefer football. What is your name?'

Sanjay came to know much later just how much Bimal-da liked football. This was also one of the factors that cemented his friendship with Bimal-da.

'My name is Bobby. My proper name is Sanjay.'

'When you are done playing, come to our house. We can chat for a while.'

'All right. I'll come in a while.'

Within a half hour Sanjay landed up in Bimal-da's home. He asked his wife for two cups of tea and then he started chatting with Sanjay. The latter chatted to his heart's content, sometimes about his home, about sports, sometimes about different cities. It was hard to tell that the two had just met today, a couple of hours ago! In short, they really took to each other. Sanjay seemed to find a firm ground, where every blade of grass was known to him. The scent of that soil was dear to him. The bond that was formed in 1971 stayed strong for many years. When Sanjay shifted with his family to Jamshedpur in 1992, the bonds loosened a little. The impact of Bimal-da in Sanjay's life is immeasurable. When one is stepping into adulthood, at seventeen or eighteen, one does need a person to go to with all the questions that raise their heads, that ask to be answered, about life, nature, society, and even religion and faith. In Sanjay's life that person was Bimal-da. He would not only answer queries, but he would also lend an umbrella of trust, like the wise banyan tree which provided shade and recourse to the weary traveller. Bimal-da would provide succor to the troubled mind with his discourse and his calm approach to restless questions. He provided the known quotient to many an unknown and he fielded many daily trials and tribulation with the skilled hands of a healer, putting doubts to rest and providing direction to thought.

Sanjay was aware of the kind of relationship that was described in the ancient epics and the Puranas, between a guru and his disciple. He was not exactly aware that a similar bond was being forged in his life at that moment, but he did have a sense of a momentous relationship being created.

In a similar fashion another relationship had burgeoned in his life. In the football field, he became friends with a tall, lithe young boy. He too had come to play football in the Mainul Hak Stadium. Every evening matches were played in that stadium of Rajendra Nagar. The boy was called Pulu. He lived in Bhikna Pahari. It wasn't far from Chaitolla—about ten minutes on foot. Pulu's father was a surveyor in general insurance and Pulu had three siblings: another brother and two sisters. His mother was a housewife. Although he was younger than Sanjay, they soon became fast friends.

At the age of sixteen Sanjay forged yet another close bond. A boy named Ashim who lived in the neighbourhood, became a bosom friend. Ashim's family owned their house in Chaitolla. The two storied house had a little spare ground in front, which looked like a playing field because it had a boundary wall. Sanjay and his friends played cricket there. Sometimes Satyajit too joined them. There was a road called Sayyeedpur just ahead of the Bhikna Pahari crossing, which went and joined another road at the extreme end of Rajendra Nagar. Satyajit's home was on that Sayeedpur Road. They too were three brothers. His father was an officer in the Central Excise Department and his mother was a housewife.

One day, as Sanjay was playing cricket in Ashim's home field, his eyes strayed to a room's window nearby. A young girl stood at the window. Her bespectacled eyes were gazing steadily at Sanjay. The minute their eyes met, she stirred and shifted her glance. In a short while she left the window. Sanjay realized that she had been gazing at him for a long time and she moved away as soon as their eyes met. The incident moved something deep in him.

The young girl was Mita. She was a little more than a year older than Ashim and a bit younger than Sanjay, studying a grade below him. She was in the ninth grade in Rabindra Vidyalay. Later he had studied her carefully—five feet four inches, slim and lithe, not exactly dark complexioned but a wheatish hue, and her eyes shone brightly. All in all, a strong presence. Even in regular garb, Mita impressed Sanjay greatly.

The field in t heir locality would host the annual Durga Puja. Sanjay was not particularly interested in the Puja, but the festive ambience was a magnet for him. The fact that everyone decked up in new clothes, gathered together to chat and exchange news, go about in the evenings, would be a source of joy for him. Every year for Durga Puja Sanjay would usually go with Ashim or Pulu and tour the well-known pandals of Patna city. But after the eye contact with Mita, he was loath to leave his home pandal and go anywhere, especially not for the duration of time that Mita was present in the pandal.

On the ninth day of the Puja his heart would start sinking. In the midst of the festivities galore, he would start looking glum because the very next day it would all come to an end. After the puja on the morning of the tenth day, the idol would go for immersion. Before that the women would play with sindoor. From a very young age Sanjay had found these rituals related to the worship of idols a bit childish. He could understand the meaning of meditation or a spiritual journey. But what was the purpose of handing an array of materials in front of a lifeless idol and playing at worshipping. When he had raised these questions as a grown up, the band of idolators had tried to provide their own brand of reasoning—some said it improves concentration and faith in the almighty, some said the holy books have sanctioned such rituals, and most people had said that it was a force of habit, because they had gotten accustomed to it from their childhood, they could not stop following the customs.

Whatever the answer, Sanjay never felt satisfied with it. He found most of them coming from a place of non-thinking. This breed of reasoning in fact puts the philosophy—which was the basis of it all—in question. But even in the midst of all this, the festive element of the Pujas always enthralled Sanjay. He enjoyed the spontaneous interactions between friends and family. And he enjoyed being able to gaze his fill at Mita for the five days of the Puja. He rejoiced in that meeting of four eyes, those deep glances that, without a word, conveyed a togetherness and the ripples of adulation played on the heart.

9

THE AWAKENING OF A NEW CONSCIOUSNESS

•••

Sanjay desperately needed a job. No business spawned by Baba or Kaku ever made it to stability. Both of them had tried several times after losing the hotel. Eventually they managed to acquire the contract for a canteen in a women's college in Patna. Sanjay's father with his reputation as a professional sportsman, had gained a bit of ground in certain circles in the city. A few aficionados of football had heard of Bapi Roy in Patna. There was a homeopath called Dr B. Bhattacharya. He loved football. He somehow got wind of the fact that the Bapi Roy who had played in Kolkata's Arian Club, was now in Patna. At first they made contact and later they grew quite close. Sanjay's father was also a good singer. When he sang Rabindrasangeet in his full-throated style, it was haunting and impressive. In a short while he also joined theatre circles and that got him a little more renown. With all these contacts he acquired the contract for the canteen and in the early days it began to do well. But it was an erratic income. In the summers the college and consequently the canteen would remain closed for two months. It would be the same for Durga Puja, Kali Puja, Chhat Puja—a total of about forty-five days. When the canteen was open, the household would be well-fed. The three brothers would be in the best of spirits. But when it was shut, there would be a scarcity of food. In such situations there was one household where the three brothers would gain succor. Not one of the t here would say a word. With empty stomachs, their lips would be sealed. But that house was like something from another planet. In that house everyone was delighted to just feed the three brothers.

After a few months, gradually the brothers got comfortable in that house. There is no accounting for the amount of time that the three of them spent in that house, over the years. And thus the closeness blossomed with Bimal-da. He was about twenty odd years older than Sanjay. But that never factored in the equation. The adda, or animated conversations with Bimal-da would strike up at any time and often Pulu joined in. Every morning Pulu and Sanjay would land up at Bimal-da's home. If it was a day off, there was nothing like it. But even on a working day, Bimal-da would chat for some time with both of them in the mornings. Satyajit too would join in. If not every day, at least often. An adda is incomplete without tea. Bimal-da's wife, whom they all called Mejdi, would supply endless cups of tea. In the evenings Sanjay and the lot had no truck with studies. After they were done with their round of sports, they would land up again at Bimal-da's home. Sanjay and Pulu were addicted to the playing field. In winters they sometimes gave a slip to cricket, but they never ever skipped football. Both Sanjay and Pulu were committed to football.

Meanwhile Bimal-da too would rush back home from work, change his clothes, and quickly get ready for the adda. Sanjay, Pulu and sometimes Satyajit too would land up for this adda. In a while Mejdi would bring the tea. These addas had no fixed boundaries. Anyone could strike up any topic and the adda would get rolling. Usually, it would veer around politics, economics, literature or sports. Rarely even cinema or music would feature. Primarily the discussions revolved around why the nation was in this state, why so many people were unemployed, what was the cause of the economic inequalities, and the state of education and health in the country. As these issues were discussed, the role and existence of God would also make its way into the discourse. Bimal-da was an atheist. Sanjay would often offer counter-arguments. He found it difficult to dismiss the conditioning of years. Sanjay was greatly influenced by his grandmother. He grew up sleeping beside her, listening to stories, poems, which lived in his mind. Grandmother was a great fan of Rabindranath Tagore. She could recite many of his poems by rote. So many nights he would listen to her reciting Tagore's poems as he had difficulty falling asleep.

Grandmother did not believe in ghosts. But she had complete and utter faith in God. Actually, Sanjay was born in a Brahmo household. There was no idol worship in the house, everyone believed in a single Almighty. But Sanjay's mother came from a slightly different school of thought. She, according to her faith, sometimes performed Lakshmi Puja in the house. But of course, it never brought any changed to the financial fortunes of the family. Therefore, on account of being the eldest son, Sanjay desperately needed a job.

Bimal-da had four brothers. The eldest—Khagen-da—had worked in the Indian Air Force for many years and then had been absorbed by the Central Flood Forecasting Division as an ex-serviceman. He knew all the details of Sanjay's family circumstances and he was also very fond of these three brothers. Out of empathy, he got Sanjay a job in his office as a dispatch clerk. It was a casual employment, without a written contract. His monthly salary was a hundred and seventy-two rupees. In 1972 that was not a very mean figure, especially given the family's constrained situation.

The office was close to the home. Sanjay managed to get hold of a cycle. He used that to commute to work. He was all of twenty years old. At that age, he really didn't enjoy going to work. His heart lay in the adda in Bimal-da's house or on the playing field. But there was really no choice. But of course, Khagen-da's presence in the office energized him to an extent.

After about three months Sanjay had a conflict with the boss—Tanmoy Bose—on a trifling matter. Actually, in the dispatching process, Sanjay was messing up, a bit like matching the wrong names to the wrong addresses. When Tanmoy babu got to hear of it, he summoned Sanjay and gave him a piece of his mind. In an office scenario this was nothing unusual. Seniors would routinely lecture their juniors if there was an error. But Sanjay could not accept that. He answered back and the next day, instead of letting the matter rest, he handed in his resignation letter to Tanmoy Bose. The latter was astounded! For such a trifling matter the young fellow was raising such a ruckus and actually resigning from the job. He thought of Khagen-da immediately. It was on his recommendation that Sanjay had been hired. Tanmoy babu was a little disturbed at the thought of upsetting Khagen-da. But anyway, the matter was finally taken up by Khagen-da and no one came to know of this incident in the office. But after much convincing, Sanjay refused to take back the resignation letter. So he finally quit the job. It was back to the adda, the playing field. He had lost contact with Pulu during the day—it was reestablished.

Within a short while, a chance meeting with someone for an hour, turned Sanjay's life around completely. One evening Sanjay and Pulu had gone to visit an acquaintance in the hospital. A tall, slim young man had also gone to the same hospital to visit another patient. Sanjay and Pulu's acquaintance was a nurse in the same hospital. She introduced them to this tall, lithe young man. Within a few short minutes, the young man won them over with his skill over words.

As they spoke, the young man revealed that he was familiar with Sanjay's father and Kaka. His name was Sanghamitro Sen, aka Babu. Sanjay and Pulu began to call him Babu-da. He was from Kolkata, a graduate of Calcutta University. He had broken his teeth on Marxism as a student in Vidyasagar College and later was involved in the Marxist revolution. In 1972, when all of Bengal was frothing in the throes of revolution and the student population was dreaming of change, Babu-da too had taken the plunge and joined the waves of revolt. He was not an extremist by ideology, but he did believe strongly in the anti-establishment movement for change. After going underground for quite a while, he escaped to Patna. Babu-da's wife's sister and her husband lived right behind the Golghar of Patna. Babu-da had taken refuge in a tiny room on the first floor of their house. The area was called Mandiri.

Very soon after making Babu-da's acquaintance, Sanjay and Pulu became regular visitors. The distance between Chaitolla and Mandiri was hefty, almost five kilometres. But the magnetism of Babu-da made it all seem worthwhile. Every day a new topic would grace the table. When Babu-da began t o hold forth on philosophy, the two boys listened attentively. The discourse ranged from Dvaita-Advaita, Ved-Vedanta-Upanishads to Dialectical Materialism. Sanjay and Pulu had a nodding acquaintance with these topics, but not enough to go deep and engage in dialogue, and certainly not with someone who had accumulated knowledge as carefully as Babu-da.

There were many things that they enjoyed discussing, and then there were topics that left them cold or uncomfortable. For example, Vedanta claims that the world is an illusion. Babu-da would argue that this insight too has taken shape within that illusionary world and in that case, isn't it a moot point? There were many other such topics under discussion, such as 'there's no such thing as a soul', 'there is nothing after death, just one life and one death' etc. Sanjay and Pulu would find such points hard to digest. They would have a hundred questions for Babu-da. But on the face of the older man's well-considered opinions and arguments, they would hold their peace. In this manner, one day the topic of mind and matter came up.

Babu-da asked, 'Tell me boys, what comes first—mind or matter?'

Sanjay and Pulu fell from the sky. What kind of a question was this?

They were of one opinion—mind of course. Matter was lifeless, without consciousness. Mind could think, it was conscious, it could compute. This was an open and shut case. It was the mind that had given birth to so many different forms of matter. How could matter supersede mind? Babu-da heard them out intently, and then he said, 'Millions and billions of years ago, was there life on earth? There wasn't. But matter still existed, in varied forms and varied shapes. The mind came into existence after the advent of life. The "mind" of today has undergone many stages of evolution and then come to this point.'

But the boys could not be convinced. They asked, 'But all these material things, some useful, some superfluous, have they all created themselves?'

'Certainly the utilitarian objects have all been created due to the workings of the mind. The evolved mind analyses, perceives and discovers. But matter has been in existence even before the mind. And therefore. Matter comes before the mind.'

Sanjay and Pulu had difficulty accepting this. They fell in deep thought—they'd never thought of it this way before. Such statements shook the very foundation of their belief system. Sometimes they felt ire against Babu-da. They felt like never seeing him again. But they couldn't; Babu-da spoke words, evinced such opinions that were very true to life. His words revealed such truths that touched life very closely. So, an irrevocable attraction drew them towards him again and again.

Within a few months, a lot of changes came over Pulu and Sanjay. They read many books during this time. If at first they couldn't make sense of it, they read them again. Sometimes they discussed amongst themselves. Satyajit, and sometimes Bimal-da too, participated in these discussions. Bimal-da often shared with them some of his life experiences and some theoretical viewpoints. It served to enrich their discussions. Gradually, the little bundle of historical and dialectical materialism began to come apart and reveal itself to their mindscapes. It was as if a hitherto-difficult mathematical equation was gradually becoming lucid and solvable.

They had heard that change is inevitable. Everything was subject to change. Over the course of time this eternal truth began to reveal itself to them. They realized that matter, consciousness, the body, the mind, and even nature was in a constant process of change. The form and speed of change may vary—but change in itself was inevitable. There was no exception to this rule.

It was the era of Indira Gandhi in Delhi. The entire nation was bubbling over with rebellion and public ire. The youth had no jobs. Farmers were in a pitiable state. The entire political system was corrupt at the roots. To add to the misery, the prices of daily necessities were shooting up at an alarming rate. In 1973, students and youth launched the Nav Nirman movement in Gujarat. That movement cast its shadow on the entire country, including Bihar. The Bihar Chhatra Sangharsh Samiti was formed. On 18 March 1974 they sent out a call for gherao of the Bihar Legislative Assembly. They had four main demands: the resolution of unemployment, inflation, crime and corruption and the irregularities in the education system. The movement took the whole of Bihar by storm. The then-

Chief Minister, Abdul Ghaffar Khan, failed to control them despite all his efforts.

On 18 March Patna was transformed into a war zone. Thousands of students and youth were vying to enter the Assembly premises. Meanwhile, large numbers of CROF soldiers and police had been posted to prevent just such an eventuality.

Sanjay, Pulu and Bimal-da had stepped out. Headed towards these agitations. When they reached Dak Bungalow, they found utter chaos. A bunch of students had coopted a few state buses and were driving around on the road while police forces were chasing them with batons. They came to know that a few student leaders had been wounded by police batons and in turn, their stones pelted by them had wounded a few policemen.

A little distance from Dak Bungalow stood a newspaper office. This newspaper was in the habit of singing in praise of the government. In front of their eyes, a few men began to pelt stones upon the door of this newspaper office.

They came to know that a telephone exchange a short distance away had already been set on fire. All in all, it was a terrible situation. It was impossible to proceed further on Bailey Road. A little further down, near the High Court, police were milling around in throngs. Police vehicles were whizzing on the roads everywhere.

After standing at the Dak Bungalow crossing for some time, Sanjay and party decided to push forth. Under the circumstances, they decided to give Bailey Road the skip and proceed by the R-Block Road towards the Assembly. As one set off on Bailey Road from Dak Bungalow, there was a narrow lane on the left. That lane wound its way towards Mithapur, The locality was called Bandar Bageecha. But even that approach was crowded to the gills that day. Perhaps everyone had the same idea of skipping Bailey Road and reaching R-Block via Bandar Bageecha. Sanjay and party joined the crowds and began to walk slowly as part of the crowd.

They had barely walked fifty metres along that road when they came upon a bunch of policemen—about ten of them. Their uniform indicated that they were probably CRPF. They were charging with their batons raised and they were lashing out at anyone who came in their way. It took them a while to take stock of the situation. When the raised baton was ten feet away from Bimal-da, he yelled, 'Run for your life.'

The words fell on them like a whiplash. Sanjay and the others turned around and began to run. The policemen saw them running and began to run after them. When they realized that, Sanjay and his friends accelerated their speed. At the time Sanjay and Pulu were regulars on the football field and they had immense faith in their athletic prowess. They were only worried about Bimal-da. He was much older, and a smoker at that. Would he succeed in running fast and escaping the police?

Wonder of wonders, when they had run quite a distance, slid into a narrow lane and stood there panting, Bimalda stood in an adjoining lane, waving at them. He was breathing absolutely normally, with no sign of strain—after running almost thirty metres alongside them.

Sanjay still remembers that incident. He recollected many such tales of Bimal-da's bravery. Once apparently, Bimal-da had jumped out of a moving train when it failed to stop at that station. And on another day, the three of them had gone to watch a football match in an enclosure in Gandhi Maidan. Two famous teams of Patna were to play that day. The place was crowded as hell. A section of Gandhi Maidan had been closed off with asbestos sheets, which was called an enclosure. Within that the first division football league matches were held. Only a section of the crowds had been able to make their way into the enclosure that day. The larger majority, not being accommodated, stood on a hillock just outside the enclosure, watching the match from there. There was much pushing, shoving, and jostling in this crowd. In the course of the match, at a moment of excitement, the crowd that stood at the back fell upon the crowd in the front. Unable to control themselves, this huge multitude fell forward and crashed into the enclosure wall, which in turn collapsed upon the viewers seated inside. It so happened that Sanjay and his friends were standing right there and so they were crushed under that collapsing asbestos wall. Although not serious, there were some injuries for sure. Cuts and bruises and some bleeding.

At the sight of this mayhem, Bimal-da—although not gravely injured himself—lost his cool. He stood up on that fallen enclosure wall and roared like a lion. That roar made the entire crowd disappear in one-minute flat! That was the day Pulu and Sanjay had witnessed the fiery face of Bimal-da—what an intrepid soul. What rage, what a roar. And many months later, on 18 March, they gained in Bimal-da a runner par excellence too.

The age at which a growing adult matured into an experienced adult through a rite of passage, absorbing insights gained from experiences and contact with other people, was the same as when Sanjay came in contact with Bimal-da. Often Sanjay wondered, if he hadn't met Bimal-da what would have happened? Would he be a different person then? Moulded by different ways of thinking and conditioned differently? Would he be like others around him, self-absorbed and self-serving?

On further thinking, he realized that it was not that simple. There were many factors involved in a person's growing up—some of it was subjective and some of it was objective. Perhaps the objective factors comprised the greater share. But yes, certain people and certain events performed a catalytic role in the process of evolution of a human mind. Bimal-da occupied such a place in Sanjay's life.

And Babuda—who ignited the spark in Sanjay's conflagratory mind. And that happened during the student movement of 1974.

After seeking and receiving many answers, he had placed his impoverished life under the microscope and scanned it diligently. He had retrieved those answers again and again in the writing of Victor Hugo, Manik Bandopadhyay, Nikolai Ostrovsky and Maxim Gorky. Sanjay had tried to solve the unsolved equations of his life patiently. So much so that the day Mita turned down his proposal humbly, his soul had been temporarily shrouded in darkness, but soon he had taken heed of the solution to the incomplete equation, in the realization that without financial independence life remained incomplete and unresolved. His first love required to be sacrificed at the altar of that insight.

He remembered that day clearly. In a short letter, he had laid his heart bare to Mita. That declaration was shrouded in hesitation and doubt. And that was because of the gap in the social and economic statuses of the two families. The perception of that gap had occupied all the space in Sanjay's consciousness. And it had left its imprint on that five-sentence note bearing the message of his heart. Of course, Mita had honoured his sentiments but conveyed her rejection in a four-sentence response to that note.

Much later, when his realization of the nitty gritty of life's reality was complete, then through the haze of emotion and feeling, he emerged a wiser soul. He understood that the fate of his 'first love' was preordained and inevitable. Like many other chapters of his life, this one too lay itself before Sanjay's analytical gaze. Although, the memories and the feelings associated with the 'first love' of one's life perhaps remained indelible in every mind.

10

TURBULENT TIMES

•••

That movement of 1974 eventually swelled and spread. The agitation of the students against the Bihar Government got transformed into a mass movement against the Indira Gandhi Government. Though the epicentre was Patna, the leadership of Jaya Prakash Narayan took it beyond the boundaries of Bihar thereby influencing the entire country. Blinded by impetuosity, in June 1975, Indira Gandhi retaliated by decreeing the Emergency. Inexplicably harsh laws were enforced, Opposition leaders were packed in jails, agitators were mercilessly hounded by the police and the intelligence. It seemed that absolutism was hellbent on unleashing a reign of terror on the people. Independent

India had never faced such an abominable governance before.

Like every action begetting an opposite reaction, the excesses of Emergency gave rise to unprecedented anti-government sentiments. The torturous Indira regime united the Opposition. Setting aside their differences, the Opposition came together to form a new party. The seething anger against the Indira Government provoked many, who otherwise kept away from politics, to come out in the open.

It was in such a turbulent time that Sanjay responded to his inner call and joined a Leftist Organization. His mind then was desperately seeking solutions to the plethora of inequalities that plagued the society. At this juncture, he found Pulu beside him. Satyajit was close to both. Notwithstanding his awkwardness that distanced him from the activities, they shared the same outlook. Different from the contemporary careerist youth, they could not keep themselves insulated from the simmering world outside. That was why the trio and Bimal-da became mutually very close.

For Sanjay, it was like entering a never before world where material pleasures peeled off before the pulsating aura of idealism. A devoted Marxist willingly relinquishes his home, property, job, family and even his life. Yet they are often derided as Materialists by those who on the other hand remain embedded in materialistic pleasures without any sense of idealism or the need for it. For them, the question of giving up all is a quixotic proposition.

People smirk at Marxists as materialists. They feel they are head over heels in love with materialism! But in actuality, barring a few, the majority often fail to distinguish between materialism and material pleasure.

However, Sanjoy was undergoing a rapid change. In every topic a new thought kept on blooming within him. More often than not, they were completely in disarray with the old beliefs. Babuda's words revisited him those days. While arguing with Babuda, there were many things which Sanjay found hard accept to accept. Now they all seem so logical and appropriate.

Sanjay completed his B.com amidst that melee. His preparation was pathetic but Satyajit's notes were of great help. They enabled him to wade through the examination successfully. The party activities started in full swing. At home, the incessant teething of scarcity went on as always. His brothers continued their studies in whatsoever manner. Sometimes the admission fees for college could not be gathered. More often than not, the tuition charges could not be paid. It was impossible to think of buying textbooks. The lady's canteen barely managed to run which somehow provided the seven their daily bread. Anything else was a luxury.

During those days their uncle landed a job as an accountant in a refrigeration company. The salary, though meagre, meant much to the family. Notwithstanding such glaring poverty, the three brothers kept on with their studies. Their keen desire coupled with their mother's role was responsible for the wonder. Neighbours and friends lent sympathetic support to their struggle. Their maternal aunts also stood beside them during those times of extreme hardship.

As the saying goes, every chapter comes to its unavoidable conclusion. The same happened to that episode in Sanjay's life. However, it was not without the proverbial twist in the tale. A massive twist it was indeed! Neither his mother nor anyone else had ever hindered Sanjay's political forays. Ma herself made eatables for the young party workers. She knew well that the boys often arrived hungry. They were a brilliant lot who had joined the party with the dream of transforming the society. They also called her- Ma, an endearing address that soothed her beyond words. Compromising on her own food, mother often used to feed them. The boys too had tremendous affection for her.

However, mother always reminded Sanjay of her fondest wish- her son would complete his studies and settle in a posh job and uplift the financial condition of the family. Every now and then, whenever opportunity presented itself, she would ask Sanjay

"Won't you look for a job?"

Sanjay usually kept quiet. Sometimes he answered, "No, not now. Don't you see the wretched condition of the country? This requires a drastic change. So, I am working for the party now."

Without further ado, mother used to fall silent.

Sanjay secured his B. Com degree in 1975.Set to be completed a year ago, Jaya Prakash Narayan's clarion call to students to join the movement caused the delay. JP wanted students of colleges and universities to sacrifice a year and they enthusiastically responded. The institutions were forced to wear a deserted look. Patna University deferred all its examinations by a year.

Another year passed. Mother did not raise the issue of job. However, from the early days of 1977, she repeatedly reminded Sanjay of the same. Sanjay was twenty-four years old then. Mother was apprehensive that within a few years, he would become over-aged for employment. Banks and insurance companies were hiring then and twenty-five was the cut-off age for the post of a clerk. The financial alarm bell was ringing loud and clear within their family. Sanjay decided to present the delicate situation to his party.

His party members were no strangers to Sanjay's household woes. It was quickly ascertained that Sanjay required to crack a job quickly through appropriate preparation. A professional could still serve the party afterwards. Few books were hurriedly gathered. Sanjay started to utilise an hour and a half from his party engagements for the preparation.

Within five to six months three banks announced vacancies through newspapers. Examinations were scheduled after three months. A successful written test was to be followed by an interview. A medical test would ultimately clinch the employment.

The written part was duly held for the three and Sanjay qualified in two of them. One interview was promptly taken and Sanjay crossed that hurdle too. He waited with mixed emotions for the posting.

Meanwhile a party programme cropped up. Indira Gandhi was arriving at Patna. She was to be greeted with black flags. By then Indira had become an ex-Prime Minister, having suffered a landslide defeat in the 1977 general elections. The Janata Dal was in power and Morarji Desai was the new Prime Minister. Yet the despotic Indira had to be reminded that Patna was reluctant to forgive her draconian reign. Thus unforgiving black flags would jeer her in the Patna airport itself.

The preparations followed accordingly. It was chalked out that on the morning of 9 April, Sanjay and others would arrange a crowd of thousands comprising youth, students and slum-dwellers. By half past nine they would reach the airport. They would erupt into slogans and flag-waving the moment Indira's flight landed. During those days, there were some big and small slums on the eastern part of Patna. Sanjay and Ashok used to work among those ricksaw and cart-pullers, plumbers, sweepers and other marginalized sections of the society. Connecting their everyday reality with political consciousness, efforts were sincerely made to educate this faction appropriately. This was an extremely important endeavour. The proletariat had to be roused with care so that they embraced Marxism and become effective agents in ushering the revolution.

The slum-dwellers, still licking the wounds of Emergency, responded to the campaign with gusto. The student and youth organizations were asked to pull up their socks for the showdown.

On 9 April, the activists took position outside the arrival zone of the Patna airport. The area was already swarming with Congressmen, their flags, banners and festoons. Evidently, Indira Gandhi was to be given a heroic welcome. Sensing this, Sanjay's team moved towards them. Within minutes the face-off happened. Pro-Indira and anti-Indira slogans were exchanged initially. The situation was rapidly getting volatile. Suddenly the flag sticks started to rain down on the opposing group. Some in Sanjay's group were badly injured. Taken aback by the violence, the slum people fled in panic while the students tried to resist. Sanjay took shelter behind an ambassador. Suddenly he saw, Ananda, a prominent member of their leadership, cornered by few men. Sanjay ran towards his distressed comrade only to be graced with a personal disaster. They pulled him down and incessant fists and kicks followed. Sanjay's face quickly got distorted. Warm blood oozed down from the corner of his eye. He felt the menacing touch of a sharp metal on his right wrist. Within seconds, a red sprout was formed and Sanjay got lost in darkness.

Almost three hours had passed before Sanjay regained consciousness in the surgical ward ICU of the Patna Medical College and Hospital. Drip on left hand, pain shooting through his body, the bandaged right hand sending distress signals—it was a harrowing experience.

Mother came to his bedside after few minutes. Her eyes were brimming with tears. Ma lightly rested her right hand on Sanjay's forehead. As remembrances gradually returned, Sanjay felt acutely worried about the predicament of others.

Slowly, mother enlightened him about the ruckus. Ananda and Selim were also admitted there. Ananda had got his collar bone broken while Selim received severe injuries on his skull. Both were on the other side of the same ICU. Though the injuries were not life-threatening, they still had to remain in the intensive care for two or four days.

After two more days, information came to Sanjay. Ananda was pinned to the ground and violently beaten with sticks. Such a blow proved too much for his collar bone. Selim meanwhile had tried to shield Sanjay from fatal consequences. In the skirmish, a dagger was swished at Sanjay. Selim intervened and took the blow on himself. The blade hit Selim's head hard and probably slipped and settled on Sanjay's right wrist. It was a grave injury resulting in huge blood loss.

After a week they were released from the hospital. Rest was understandably advised. Lying at home, Sanjay learnt that the political society of the city was raising a great hue and cry about that unprecedented manifestation of violence.

There was no choice for Sanjay but to take the much-needed rest. During those days, Pulu, Satyajit and some other members of the party used to visit him. Their company, as always, cheered him up. The wrist was recuperating well. Only the black spot below the eye stubbornly remained. It was too blatantly visible on his face.

On the afternoon of 20 April, a registered letter announced its arrival. Mother was elated to see the postman. Curiosity slowly left Sanjay's initial indifference behind.

"Was it a letter from a bank?" he wondered. It was time indeed for that interview result.

The envelope had the name of Sanjay Ray. It also bore the name of a bank. Mother hastily signed the receipt and handed the envelope to Sanjay. Sanjay opened it and found the appointment letter. He was supposed to report at the Sherghati branch of the bank on 26 April 1978. Sherghati was not very far from Gaya.

Tears of happiness welled in mothers' eyes. Sanjay saw it and failed to restrain his own eyes from brimming over. Had their struggle against penury come to an end? Was the dark night finally over? The son and his mother searched for the answer in each other's arms.

Thoughts crowded in Sanjay's mind. The challenges of a new engagement and the new place bothered him little. His mind refused to reconcile with the reality of leaving Patna. How could he sever his attachment with his dear city, his friends and party comrades. It was an excruciating emotional torture, perhaps similar to what Shakuntala had felt when she left her forest-dwelling home and went away to her husband's house.

11

LURED BY LIVELIHOOD

...

On 26 April, Sanjay joined the Shergathi branch. Along with the manager B.K.Sen, the office, which was beside the G.T.Road, had a modest manpower of around eight people. Sanjay found the summer unrelenting. It was only April and the rising mercury left Patna way behind.

Barring manager Sen, the only other Bengali there was Anindya Sarkar. He was from the Nadia district of West Bengal. Sanjay found a room for himself in the house where Anindya lived as a tenant. The landlord, an affluent local man, let out his rooms only for bank employees. The monthly rent was Rs 45.

Sanjay had only a small suitcase. Thus, the tiny room did not pose much of a problem. A medium-sized charpoy was fortuitously secured free of cost. Three rooms stood in a row. In front, there was a wide verandah. The inmates mostly preferred to place their charpoys in the verandah and enjoy a comfortable midsummer night sleep. The breeze picked up steadily as the night progressed, thereby assuring a pleasant slumber.

Sanjay woke up early. Putting on a shirt, he sauntered out. A meandering road, branching off from the G.T.Road had entered the village. Adjacent to it, the pucca houses and the mud dwellings co-existed amicably. Among them, one small building was their office. The area nearer to the GT Road was Nayabazar while the distant one was called Golabazar. Behind their office building, a river was supposed to flow, but the enervating end of April had left it absolutely high and dry. It was typical of the Gaya district—rivers without water and hills without trees!

Having satisfied himself with a functional awareness about Sherghati, Sanjay returned an hour and a half later. Anindya was up already. Sipping tea, they got engaged in gossip.

There was little to do in the office. By four in the afternoon the daily chores got done. Leaving the manager and the accountant to complete some necessary formalities, Sanjay and Anindya tried to wander here and there. However, it was more a ritual than pleasure. The place itself had painfully little to offer in terms of social life. Anindya, by virtue of his one year's experience, had made some acquaintances. Sanjay accompanied him to those places, but it was a mere speck in comparison to his pulsating Patna days. His mind incessantly yearned for Patna, his friends and family members. At work, often Sanjay sensed an emptiness within. A crushing blankness seemed to overpower the sense of smugness usually in sync with being employed. Sanjay had earlier heard about punishments of deportation beyond the seas. Likewise, he found himself marooned at Sherghati.

Somehow surviving the bland five-day ordeal, every Saturday, Sanjay took the Gaya-bound bus and boarded the evening train for Patna. Reaching there by quarter past eight, Sanjay tried to extract as much as possible from the late Saturday evenings. He spent the entire day likewise every Sunday and at night returned to Gaya via train around half past eleven. Those nights were spent at the station itself till the five o' clock morning bus took him to Sherghati.

Weeks ticked away in that manner. Sometimes mid-week holidays were also promptly utilized for Patna visits. It was almost six months when Sanjay met Rajib at a shop in Nayabazar. Longtime residents of Sherghati, where his father was a physician, Rajib was the second-born in his family. His elder brother was also a medical student while the younger was studying B.A.at Gaya College.

Though gentle and soft-spoken, Rajib was commendably appreciative. He and Sanjay quickly became friends. When Sanjay exchanged news and views about the world at large with him, Rajib listened with rapt attention. As they got closer, Sanjay started to frequent his house. He was warmly welcomed there. It was as if an over-fatigued traveller staggering across an endless, enervating desert, had suddenly discovered an oasis! Whenever Sanjay went there for a hearty evening gossip invariably, Rajib's mother would request him to stay back for dinner. It was a relief to skip the roadside hotel meal. Staying away from home for the first time, Sanjay was acutely missing the culinary delicacies of his thammi and mother and also their reassuring warmth. At Sherghati, this blankness to some extent was lessened by the endearing concerns of Rajib's mother. Understandably, Sanjay developed a keen attachment with that family.

Two and half years later Sanjay was transferred to Patna. He felt over the moon. At last his exile was over and he would be back to his world, his people and ambience. However, the ecstasy was somewhat sobered, as the transfer forced Sanjay to bid adieu to Rajib and his family. He would sorely miss them, especially the ever-caring presence of Rajib's mother.

The Patna Regional Office was also the Administrative Headquarters of the Bank. It supervised the activities of all the branches in Bihar. The Regional Manager was in charge. He also had a sizeable team of efficient subordinate officers as well as several clerks. However what irked Sanjay was the state of the Office Union. At Sherghati its influence was miniscule. Here three Unions jostled against each other. Two of them were Left-minded while one steered clear from any political influence. Yet, its leadership comprised some followers of the Socialist Party. They were quite indulgent towards the management.

At Sherghati, Sanjay had taken the membership of a Leftist Union. In Patna, they were outnumbered by the pro-management faction. Sanjay knew for sure that he had join a group. Otherwise, it would be difficult to thrive in this sector. Any demand, however just, would never stand a chance, without a workers' union supporting it appropriately. Moreover, Sanjay disliked being in isolation. So he had to make a choice.

At Sherghati, there was little scope for meaningful union-related activities beyond the formality of membership. In his new office, Sanjay settled for the group which matched his ideology and work ethic.

Slowly, Sanjay got involved with the acts and deeds of the union. It was a challenge to shoulder even the petty duties of that small group. He decided not to shy away from such opportunities. He had informed his party earlier. They too agreed that working at the banking sector, it would make no sense at all to avoid unions. The comparatively better should be chosen and meaningful political culture would emanate from it. In the process, Sanjay got close to quite a few good men. They had singular thoughts and opposed the anti-people policies of the government. Their struggle was against the anti-employee mentality and autocratic decisions of the management. The management's indifferent imposition of decisions upon the employees was absolutely unacceptable. Sanjay's cherished principles were bolstered by such stances and he participated eagerly in the agitations. Sanjay felt buoyed by the fact that he was not working only to make ends meet but serving a greater cause.

Swarup Mallick, a few years his junior, became Sanjay's close friend. Swarup was smart and suave and his actions complemented his words wonderfully. Adept at giving speeches, Swarup wrote well and was good at raising slogans too. Every now and then, agitations based on relevant issues were organized in front of the main entrance. On such occasions, a fascinated Sanjay steadfastly stared at him while Swarup continued to mesmerize his audience with superb slogans and short, purposeful speeches.

Swarup was also highly influenced by Sanjay. As their association became stronger, they started to shoulder many responsibilities of the union. Anath Chakraborty, who was in the Ranchi branch, benefited immensely from their camaraderie. Based at Ranchi, he had to look after all the units in Bihar. His workload was considerably eased by the two energetic young men, especially in Patna. The city being the state capital had its own importance. The administrative head was present here and so was the regional office. In short, Patna was the epicentre of all union-related activities for its members. Sanjay also rose in importance through his posting at the Regional Branch.

After a year or two, another bright individual got a transfer to Patna from Calcutta. A little senior to Sanjay, Barun Mishra was an accomplished young man. Having spent the first few days of his career in Calcutta, Barun was well conversant with the plans and programme of the union. Sanjay and Swarup were elated to find Barun and very soon the trio became a force to reckon with for the management. They started to visit branches strewn across Bihar with the mission of influencing the employees to join their organization. They earned the sobriquet of 'The Three Musketeers' and became very popular among the staff.

Things were getting on smoothly, when an incident stirred the hornet's nest. In those days everywhere the Bank Unions enjoyed considerable clout. With Calcutta leading the way, Trade Unionism throughout the eastern part of India was growing from strength to strength. Along with sloganeering, sit-in -protests, deputations, posters were regularly put up within and outside the branches. These posters ranged from movement -related issues to news of conferences held by the organizations.

A poster on similar lines was once printed by Sanjay's association and he himself pasted it inside the office. By no means was it something unprecedented, as previously on one or two occasions posters had adorned the walls of their office. However the unexpected resistance came from the Regional Manager himself. In an inexplicable show of anger he decreed that all posters should be taken off immediately.

Sanjay was in no mood to oblige. Rather, he tried to sense the rationale behind such rashness. He also discussed the matter with Barun and Swarup.

Several discussions ensued. Gradually it was learnt that a few days ago there was a tiff between the manager and Sanjay over an issue. The argument got increasingly unpleasant. Eventually, the manager relented with visible reluctance. The poster incident was his way of settling the score.

It was unanimously decided that posters would not be removed, irrespective of consequences. The management was duly informed. Amusingly enough, the other two unions indirectly gratified the management's ego through their acts of conformation. One group stuck their poster outside while the other agreed to peel off their poster from the office room. Thus, with Tom and Dick consenting, Harry had to wage a lone battle.

The mounting pressure failed to unsettle Sanjay and his companions. They stood their ground while the authorities kept searching for the opportunity to retaliate.

One day, Sanjay reached office ten minutes late. He was yet to master his newly purchased bike. The crowd was also a bit heavier than usual. Though such late arrivals were commonplace and usually overlooked, Sanjay was not allowed to join office on that day. Sanjay had no choice, but to enter the Regional Manager's chamber to secure the permission. In a normal situation, he often received the courteous invitation to take a seat. The treatment was palpably different that day. Pretending to be enormously preoccupied, the manager clearly stated his helplessness in the matter.

A visibly shocked Sanjay voiced his anguish before leaving the chamber-

'You are welcome to show off your power and serve justice to an individual using the office rules as an excuse. Our struggle for justice and impartiality will nevertheless continue.'

The management quickly framed a case. Two witnesses were arranged against Sanjay. A letter was sent to him citing the altercation that happened followed by a stern reprimand for his behaviour. Lastly the letter declared that Sanjay was being transferred to the Patna City branch for his actions.

A peon delivered the letter to Sanjay's table in a sealed envelope. Sanjay was at a loss! He had never wanted to work at the city branch and that seemed unavoidable from the next day. He could not fathom why such a trivial issue was blown out of proportions! Or was it a way of settling scores for the poster incident? Perhaps, the explanation lay there!

Sanjay spent some months at the city branch before he was called back. No, not the Regional Office again. The Patna Branch was to be his new work address. All harrowing notwithstanding, Sanjay happily discovered that

Barun and Swarup were in there too! Taken aback by the abrupt turn of events, a listlessness had crept in. However, with the trio coming together again, Sanjay regained his lost vigour. His presence was once again felt in programmes, strikes, agitations and protest campaigns organized by the union. Sanjay relished the charm inherent within these activities. He always maintained that such actions required both capability and devotion.

Sanjay had often perceived that people harbored an extremely unflattering opinion about unions. They considered it to be a menial engagement. Union members were generally looked down upon and branded as opportunists. Nothing could be further away from the truth. Admittedly, few individuals work to increase their personal gains. But they are overwhelmingly outnumbered by those who tirelessly toil for the greater benefit and the greater cause. They do not bother even to risk their lives. They were a well-educated, intelligent and intrepid lot. Fluent speakers with appreciable talent at writing, they held effortless conversations with eminent politicians and officials. The leadership of the unions in the banking sector was so erudite, that had they desired, they would not have found it difficult to become doctors, engineers or professors.

Thus, Sanjay had no feelings of inferiority. He cared little about the careerists. The careerists had shamelessly taken all they could from society only for themselves and their families. They thought of nothing else. Unlike their leadership, these careerists possessed no idea about the contemporary world. They were equally insouciant about their own country and countrymen.

Sanjay, however, was much distressed about a matter concerning the union. In the union meetings, enthusiasm often spilled helter-skelter whenever salary demands were discussed. The enormous amount of time and energy invested in such matters stood in stark contrast to the conspicuous absence of meaningful meetings related to the maladies plaguing the society. Redressing such ills, consequently remained a distant dream. Such lackadaisical attitude of the union in this respect relegated Lenin's doctrine of emergence from a 'class in itself' to a 'class for itself'—an untried theoretical statement.

On 26 April, 1983, Sanjay tied the nuptial knot with Mili. The marriage was arranged through party sources. Mili's father was a supporter of the party. He worked at Telco in Jamshedpur. In 1979 he suffered a fatal accident within the factory. Mili's family plunged into a grave financial crisis. They had to leave the office quarters and shift to someone else's house. Mili's elder brother was only twenty-three then.

In a space of four or five months, Bablu was accepted as his father's replacement by the company. The relatives were extremely supportive during the interim period. It took a long time for Mili and her family to overcome the bereavement. Her mother could never retrieve her composure completely though she felt a lot relieved after Mili's marriage.

There were many twists and turns in the tale of Mili and her family. When the country was partitioned, her family had to leave behind all their possessions and assets in East Pakistan and come across the border. Mili's grandfather—Sri Surendranath Dhar—left Narayanganj, Dhaka in 1950 with his entire family and was forced to take refuge in Kolkata's Taltola. Later they built a house in Birati and moved there permanently. Out of the eight brothers and three sisters, Mili's father—Sri Satyabrata Dhar—was the fifth. Early in his life he secured a job in the tea estates of North Bengal and moved there. Later he was compelled to leave his job since he came in the black book of his employer, probably for being an active member of the worker's union. After spending some time in Kolkata, someone tipped him off and he went to Jamshedpur. There he applied in Telco for a job. In 1955 he got married to Bela, the fifth child of Kamini Ghosh who lived in Uttarpara.

He worked in Tata Motors diligently for many years and acquired quite a reputation for his sincerity and abilities. On the other hand, gradually he grew conscious of bringing about changes in society. In the 1970s, when the air was heavy with revolt and rebellion, some of it rubbed off on the Dhar family as well. Actually, there was good reason for Mili's father's left-centric position. One of his older brothers, Sudhin Dhar, was an active member of the Communist movement. He had been jailed in the Rajshahi jail in 1950, along with many other communist rebels. At the time, they had revolted against the pathetic quality of food served in prisons. On 24 April, the prisoners were subjected to merciless gunfire. Sudhin Dhar and seven other rebels died in that incident. This caused a furore in Bengal and in many other parts of the country. Quite naturally, Mili's father was deeply influenced by his brother and therefore he dreamed of changing society. For the same reason he was greatly empathetic towards the young men who lived with similar dreams and who gave up their homes, comforts, jobs and devoted their lives to resisting the establishment. In this fashion, he became a member of the Party and a very close associate of those young men.

There's no count of the number of Party members who visited the two-roomed home of Telco, where they discussed Party ideology and its workings till well into the night. Mili's mother would be asleep in the other room with her children. Sometimes some of these discussions fell in her ears as well. Even if she didn't comprehend everything, she could tell one thing for sure—these young souls had many dreams. They spoke of nurturing such a world where there would be no poverty, no unemployment and no inequality. Where everyone would be assured of food, shelter, education and health. Where there would be no worries about her son Bablu securing a job. Bablu was quite young then. He was busy with his games and studies. He was quite good at Maths. He was fond of all sports, but football was his favourite, and he was a good player. Mili loved to dance. Her parents wanted her to focus on it. They enrolled her for dance classes. Initially her mother used to take her to class. This would really motivate Mili and she gave her everything to learning dance. As she grew older, she began to go alone for the classes. Within a few years

Mili learned to dance quite well. She continued with it along with her studies.

Mili's father was a bookworm. He was a member of the local library too. When he came back from work, he would freshen up and sit down with a book. Mili's mother would serve him tea. Telco was a very pretty locale by itself. It had all the bounties of nature, situated as it was on the eastern fringes of Jamshedpur. A little township that was picture perfect. As far as the eye could see, there was greenery and the Dolma mountains lay spread out. The roads were smooth and tarred as they wound their way through the township. The avenues were lined with Gulmohur, Radhachura and many other flowering trees. When dusk yielded to evening, Telco looked all decked up in the fancy street lights installed by the company. Mili's father was a nature lover. He loved gardening. In the strip of land in front of their quarters, he grew a varied range of plants. The tiny family of parents and two children were a portrait of joy and bliss.

Two young men from the Party were regulars in their home—Shyamal and Nantu. Shyamal was from Jamshedpur. He had gone to Kolkata for higher studies and gotten involved with politics. Nantu had run away from Kolkata and sought refuge in Jamshedpur. They got along very well with Mili's mother. They would plead for many kinds of dishes, and she too enjoyed making them and feeding the two boys.

In the early part of 1982, Sanjay had come to Jamshedpur for a friend's wedding. He had visited the place earlier too. But he had never liked the township as much before as he had on that trip. He had mulled over the idea for many months. He felt that the town had a good mix of middle-class residents. It also had a vibrant political scene where the Party was quite active and visible. So one day he spoke his mind to Nantu and the others, 'If there is a girl of marriageable age from the home of a Party supporter, do let me know. I wish to get married.'

In response Shyamal had said, 'We'll have to see. But surely one can be found.'

Nantu gave it a bit of thought and said, 'There is a very good girl. Her father was a Party supporter. He passed away in an accident around three years ago.'

Sanjay said, 'Do have a word with them.'

'All right, I'll do it soon,' Nantu assured him.

Within a month or so the news arrived—the girl was around twenty years old. She was doing her B.A. She lived with her mother and her older brother, who had got a job in Telco after their father passed away. Her father had been a committed supporter of the Party. He had been very affectionate towards Nantu and Shyamal and he had given them shelter in his own home during the Emergency.

All these details left a great impact on Sanjay. He became very anxious to go to Jamshedpur and meet the girl. A few weeks later the opportunity came. He had to visit Jamshedpur for some Party-related work. After finishing his work, he began to nudge Nantu to head towards Telco. Nantu was enjoying the fun. He could tell that Sanjay was dying to go and meet Mili. But he feigned innocence and stayed put even after a couple of broad hints from Sanjay. The third time Sanjay sighed and said obliquely, 'I suppose this time around I must give Telco a miss. All right, let it wait for next time.'

Nantu responded immediately, 'No, no, it must happen this time, I have kept them informed, that we'll arrive around four o'clock.'

'Oh, then we must leave right away,' Sanjay replied.

'Yes, let's go,' Nantu bade everyone goodbye and they set off. From that spot both buses and autos went to Telco. They picked an auto. Within half an hour they reached Telco, and from there it was about ten minutes on foot.

The quarters were small. There were two rooms, but quite small in size. When they rang the bell, a woman of about fifty opened the door. This was Mili's mother—Bela. She received them graciously and offered them seats in the front room. After about ten minutes Mili came in.

She had good features, a clear complexion and a headful of dark tresses. But she wasn't very tall. Sanjay liked her at first sight. He realized that she was also taking him in through stolen glances. But she wasn't saying much, apart from brief answers to the few questions that Sanjay put before her. Mili's mother placed before them two plates of vegetable chops and sweets, for Sanjay and Nantu. A little later she brought two cups of tea. When she noticed that Sanjay hadn't touched the snacks, she said,

'Why haven't you started yet? The chops are freshly fried and still hot—start before it cools.'

Sanjay and Nantu began to eat, and Mili went inside. When they had finished eating, Nantu said, 'If you two wish to talk alone, with some privacy, you can go to this little park nearby and sit and chat for some time. Let me have a word with Mili and her mother.'

And it was done. Ten minutes from Mili's home, there was a very pretty little park. Full of varied flora and decorative bushes, the pleasant park was quite empty at that time of the day. It was quite obvious that this was no playground for children. Mili said that it was mostly frequented by the elderly and seldom ever a pair of lovers would find their way into it. It was a little over five in the evening. The sun was still burning down fiercely and so, the place was free of other people. The two of them took their seats on a bench, keeping a modest distance between themselves.

After a longish pause, Sanjay asked, 'When will the final exams? start?'

Mili said, 'Next year, in January or February.'

'How are your preparations coming along?'

'So far so good.'

'Do you know everything about me?'

'Yes, I have heard,' Mili's reply was brief.

'I work in a bank.'

'I know.'

'I shall never take a promotion. I hope you have no objections to that?' He threw the question at Mili.

'No, I have no objection.' Mili's voice was firm and unwavering.

Sanjay liked this steadiness of tone in Mili. More often than not a prospective bride was curious and interested in her husband's earning and prosperity. Sanjay felt Mili was not that kind of a girl. He took the decision—if no other hitches came their way, Mili was the one for him.

On returning to Mili's home, he informed Nantu of his decision. Mili's mother was relieved and delighted. Sanjay too went back to Patna and informed his mother. She said, 'Since you have seen her and liked her, we have no further doubts. Sanjay's father, his Kaku, his thama and his younger brothers were all happy to hear the news.

The date of wedding was fixed for a few months later, after Mili completed her B.A. finals. Everyone made merry at the wedding and returned to Patna with the newly wedded Sanjay and Mili.

At first, Mili was disappointed with Patna. The hopelessly congested city seemed an eyesore in comparison with the natural abundance in Telco. In course of time, she developed a strong amity with Patna. She was delighted to get enrolled as an M.A. student at the Patna University. With acquaintances increasing, Mili was utterly thrilled by the academic standards of the much-acclaimed institution. Later, she also completed her B.Ed from the same university.

In her new household at Patna, Mili was assuredly at ease. The culture and magnanimity of Sanjay's family members acted as a positive influence on her. Mili felt a magnetic attraction towards a special member of the house. She was Sanjay's grandmother, who was called Thama. Mili had never met such a broadminded woman before. Bereft of vision in one eye, Thama defied her advanced years by sitting erect on her bed, her legs stretched wide and immersed herself in reading books indefatigably. Her memory was a veritable repository of innumerable stories and poems. The small woman never ceased to fascinate Mili. She too was extremely fond of Mili. For Thama, she was not Mili, but 'Shyamoli'. The sweetness of that call 'Shyamoli' kept ringing in Mili's ears like the lasting notes of a flute. Even after the passing away of Thama, the lingering memory of her voice continued to resonate with Mili.

12

TMH

...

Rintu and Saswata received them at the Mumbai Airport. Minutes after landing, Saswata called to inform that they were waiting outside the arrival zone. The fourteen-year-old Saswata, who looked older than his age, was Rintu's son. Somehow all of them got packed inside Rintu's car and reached his flat at Lokhandwala. It was a sprawling one, so accommodation for all was comfortably arranged.

After having lunch and a brief period of rest, the group sat down for an evening meeting. It was planned that on the next day, around half past nine in the morning, they would visit TMH. Rintu would take Sanjay, Mili, Ruhi and Badshah in his car. During registration of name at TMH, the recommendation of a doctor is desired. Rintu, aware of that, had already secured the name of a doctor working there.

The hospital was too crowded. Spread over a vast stretch of land, it consisted of three buildings. It was at Parel, a few kilometres away from Dadar. Cancer patients from every nook and corner of the country come here for treatment. Even from the neighbouring countries like Pakistan, Bangladesh, Nepal and Bhutan, people come in numbers here to avail the much-esteemed treatment, that too at such a low cost. Hordes of people throng the hospital every day. Thus the process of registration is an intimidating task that is required both for indoor and outdoor check-up. So, it took almost two hours for them to complete the relevant formalities.

Next, they went to the outdoor section of the Neurology department. The file received from the registration was submitted. They were asked to wait. Two individuals sat with a computer in a place covered on three sides. They were the ones who feed the information, as in the files, into the computer. Then, on a basis of first-come-first-serve, they forwarded the files to the doctor's chamber. Then the patients were summoned one by one to the chamber. At first, two junior doctors inspected the patient. A variety of check-ups followed. Afterwards, with their observations, they sent the patient, with the file, to the senior doctors.

Badshah too, was called in the similar process. There was a break at two o'clock that ran for half an hour. Sanjay and others kept on waiting. It was close to three o'clock when Badshah finally met the senior doctor. After going through the reports, Dr Rahul asked:

'Have you brought the block?'

'Yes, it is with us,'-Sanjay replied.

'Submit the block at the pathology department. A biopsy will be done here again.'

'What about the Columbia or NIMHANS report?'

'Apart from those, we require our own report. Treatment will start on the basis of that.'

'Well then, please tell us where the pathology department is located?'

'It is on the seventh floor of this building. For convenience, please ask the liftman.'

Dr Rahul gave a written slip and said, 'Submit the block along with this slip. Come on the 22nd. By then the report will be ready. Another MRI will follow. The course of treatment will depend on the result of the MRI.'

It took some time to locate the place. There are plenty of lifts in this hospital. Four of them are in this building. They kept on enquiring and moving accordingly. Eventually they reached the appropriate lift and arrived at the seventh floor. Walking across a waiting hall, they found a counter. None but a sullen-faced man was present there. Sanjay handed him the slip given by Dr Rahul. The man read the piece of paper and without saying anything merely raised his eyebrow.

Sanjay promptly understood that he was asking for the block. After receiving it, the man said, 'Where is the card?'

A card is given at TMH during admission. Before that, for every patient some advance has to be deposited at the cash counter. Whenever an expense is incurred within the hospital, that card is swiped to make payment. This card is known as the master card. Subsequent debits keep on decreasing the balance. Once again cash is deposited to 'recharge' the account. Sanjay gave the card. Few hours ago, he had deposited fifty thousand. The man touched the card on a machine and returned it. When asked about the delivery date of the report, he informed them that it would be sent to the neuro- outdoor. They would be informed about it there.

Once the file of a patient gets prepared, it remains stored in the related department. Relevant reports and documents shall keep on finding their place in that particular file. Every patient has an ID. Whenever required, the ID has to be stated and the computer shall provide all the information about that patient. If necessary, printed hard copy shall be handed over.

The hospital part for the day came to an end. The famished lot entered a passable eatery and gobbled toast, omelette and tea. Next, they arrived straight at home. It was touching five o' clock when, after freshening up, they sat down to lunch.

Hunger was satisfyingly resolved by rice-dal, paneer curry and salad. Rekha, an able cook, was in charge of Rintu's kitchen.

All of them, specially Badshah, required a good rest. It had been a long day from half past nine in the morning till five in the evening. Exhaustion was obvious.

Mumbai experiences late sunrise as well as sunset due to its location on the western part of India. Here the sun does not make itself conspicuous before seven in the morning and stays for another twelve hours before it decides to set. For the people from the eastern part of India, this is indeed an amazing experience.

For Sanjay, this was quite unsettling. Habitually, he got up only to meet the darkness outside. Others were fast asleep. He had no choice but to fall asleep again. In the evening, the same problem persisted. The clock showed seven yet it was not completely dark outside. Mumbai at ten or half past ten at night kept on buzzing as if dusk had just set in.

Staying for a couple of months and fifteen days, Sanjay learnt a lot from this sojourn in Mumbai. He had been to Mumbai many times before. However, those visits were like what one perceives from a first-class compartment of a running train. It was like feasting on the beauty of a city full of dreams while remaining blissfully unaware of its commoners. It was as if he was drinking the easily available purified water at home rather than venturing out to seek some unknown fountain source, discovering it braving all odds and then quenching his thirst. Along with the narrative of Badshah's treatment many more tales found their way in surreptitiously. On a July evening, Sanjay had walked past the Lokhandwala market and was nearing Charbangla when the rain came down. As the rain refused to relent, Sanjay took shelter in a bus-stand.

After sometime his eyes fell on a youth of around thirty years, who sat beside him. The young man silently gazed at the sky and kept watching the downpour.

Sanjay took the initiative and asked his name.

'Vikash,' the youth replied after a few seconds of silence.

'Where do you stay?'

Perhaps respecting Sanjay's curiosity, the young man said, 'At East Andheri here, though my home is in Bihar.'

'Where in Bihar? I had lived there too. My home was in Siwan.'

'I'm from Patna. So, Sir, you belong to Siwan?'

'Right. I had also gone to Patna many times.'

With the incessant rain helping matters, they got engaged in an amicable conversation. Sanjay told him about life at Jamdshedpur. The young man had not been to Jamshedpur. He worked as a plumber. Though his work had caught attention, he still had to look around daily for a job. It was a no work, no pay and no food situation!

'I have to dig a fresh well every day in order to drink water adequately,'

In his idiomatic expression, the young man made his desperation pretty obvious.

'Why have you come to such a faraway place leaving everything behind?'

'Sir, there is just nothing in my village. At least, here I get work and money.'

This is the reality of the country where lopsided growth has played out its worst. In some places money is being squandered for no rhyme or reason, elsewhere money has a rare enough existence. Circulation of money, to all intents and purposes, is rendered absurd by such ever-widening disparity.

Sanjay had to agree that everyone has a right to live and migration to cities thereby becomes inevitable.

For the long two months and fifteen days he was there, Sanjay used to walk around at dusk. It was an aimless sauntering that followed no particular route or sought no specific destination. Rather these ambling forays made him familiar with so many streets and lanes at Lokhandwala and Andheri West. He saw the lifestyle of those people making ends meet on the outer margins of Mumbai. Most of the day-labourers came from other states. Did they gather in Mumbai because there were no jobs in other states? Or were there other reasons? Were the people of Maharashtra not hardworking enough? Putting it another way, perhaps they disliked those jobs related to physical labour, which the Hindi-speaking community accepted readily. Did the story of Kolkata, which somewhat manifested this work-related discrimination, matched that of Maharashtra in this respect?

On 23 May, Badshah was taken to TMH again. After waiting a little while at the outdoor department, the expected call came from Dr Rahul's chamber. The biopsy report had arrived. Nothing different was discerned. The TMH report confirmed the same findings as revealed by the observations at Columbia Asia and NIMHANS. It was a grade 4 malignant tumour also known as Glioblastoma.

It meant there was no respite from worries for them. Dr Rahul said,

'Look, the MRI has to be done now as it is necessary to know the position of the tumour. I am issuing a written instruction. Take it to the MRI section and finalize the date there.'

He wrote accordingly on a piece of paper. The MRI section was on the basement floor. The technician-in-charge saw the note from Dr Rahul and said, 'Come with the patient day after tomorrow. It cannot be done before that day.'

They returned home early. It was quite obvious that MRI would be a lengthy ordeal. The section itself was a long, narrow passage teeming with people. Even during the day, the lights had to remain on. Only three MRI machines were there to meet the demands of so many patients. In comparison, Columbia Asia was not so crowded. Being a private set-up, treatment was very expensive there. Though it bore the title of Tata the TMH was governed by a public trust. It also received substantial government support. Thus at TMH treatment was much more affordable, a fact ratified by the ever-swelling number of patients. Cases of cancer are also rapidly increasing in this country of one hundred and thirty million and counting.

Not only Sanjay and Rintu, but Badshah also looked a bit concerned that day.

On 25 May, they went directly to the MRI section. The place was crowded as usual. Some had come for brain MRI, some for chest and other organs. A tedious period lapsed before Badshah's turn arrived. To undergo an MRI is not a simple matter. Laid on a stretcher, almost half of the body is put inside a machine. An overwhelming sense of suffocation sets in once the head is positioned within a dark cell. Suffocation intensifies as the X-ray machine comes down tantalizingly close to the nose. At Columbia Asia, on his very first day, Badshah had said, 'Baba, it is better to get habituated with the process of MRI.'

Badshah went inside the room without any apprehension or hesitation.

He came out almost forty minutes after. They were informed that on the next day the report would be available at the neuro outdoor.

Dr Rahul checked the MRI report and explained to them that the tumour was more or less the same as it was after the surgery. He said,

'According to us, the patient requires thirty-three sittings for radiation and as for now, forty-five oral doses of chemotherapy, each of a hundred and twenty gram. Excluding Saturdays and Sundays, radiation will be given on the other five days. However, chemo will be administered regularly."

He also pointed out that chemo and all other medicines are available in the TMH dispensary itself and should not be purchased from outside. There was no further need for outdoor visits now. After the completion of the course of radiation, another MRI would ascertain the dose and number of another round of chemo. However, radiation post-radiation, in the absence of any complication they could return to Jamshedpur. By then the doctor had come to know where they were from and also about Badshah's service in Bangalore. That day he kept on cheering Badshah, 'Young man, don't worry, you will be all right soon.'

Badshah responded with a gentle smile and said, 'Thank you.'

The radiation centre was located at the underground portion of the adjoining building. This was done as a preventive measure against the dangerous consequences of exposure to radiation.

On the first day, they found the place swarming with people. Unlike the MRI section, this centre had a large area with adequate sitting arrangements. The curious eyes of Sanjay and Mili took in the ailing multitudes who ranged from babies to octogenarians. They suffered from cancers in different parts of the body—brain, mouth, nose, throat, lungs, liver, intestine, stomach, rectum and where not! It was as if a human body was a mere microcosm of the fatal abode cancer had built for itself within mankind at large! Cancer seemed to smirk at the pride human civilization takes on itself:

'Here I am! Watch my dance of death where I merrily move from one household to another, striking at will with my fangs; catch me if you can; destroy me if you can!'

Sanjay and Mili exchanged looks. They felt they were in an alien world. The heartbeat of life was inaudible here. Instead, the throbbing of death was clear. Fear was writ large across the face of each patient. Most of them sat in silence. Closing their eyes, some of the patients rested their weary heads on the shoulders of relatives or on the laps of family members. The tiny-tots sat on their mothers' lap and kept on crying till they got worn out. They were all waiting for their turn to take the radiation. To make the waiting time bearable, a big television set was provided at a convenient level on the wall of the waiting room. However, only few patients eyed the screen. Rather, it was studiously followed by the people who accompanied the patients. For them, this waiting was an examination in itself. As each patient had to generally endure one and a half to two hours of waiting, television was the only option to kill time.

Since they reached the radiation centre, Badshah had been silent. Questions and disconcerting thoughts crisscrossed his mind. He felt like sharing the thoughts with his mother, but could not do so. Everywhere in this hospital, at every point leading from one building to another, in the distraught masses moving around, the presence of cancer patients in such formidable proportions is vehemently unsettling for anyone. However, at the radiation centre, the unnerving sensation increases by leaps and bounds. Life is forced to a halt here just like the huge traffic caught at a signal. All eyes desperately wait for the green light to set things in motion again. Similarly, at the TMH radiation centre, patients fervently wait for their recovery; enduring sitting after sitting; avidly expecting the doctor to signal the green light of release. The respite might be too short-lived, for a few months or a few years. Nevertheless, it would usher in a refreshing sense of freedom.

Badshah took some time to adjust with the environment. Initially, with questioning eyes, he looked at everything around the place. Perhaps, he found solace by seeing patients of different age groups who huddled here from different parts of the country. He realized that he was not alone in the struggle against death. There were others too waging a defiant fight against cancer. This gave him a reason to look beyond his own misery and pain.

There might be moments when queries came to his mind:- 'Why me? What have I done? I have never touched alcohol, and occasionally smoked a few cigarettes with friends in the early days of adulthood. That was all! What about those who hit the bottle regularly or those who keep on smoking one cigarette after another on a daily basis?

How many of them suffer from cancer? How many of them undergo such agony?'

Badshah knew that people would dodge the query by using words like 'fate' or 'destiny'! And the rest is silence! This is the best way to calm the tempest raging inside. Then there is God! Everything, you have to understand is 'divine desire'! Badshah was an atheist with no illusion whatsoever about the existence of God. He was aware that others might attribute the cause of his disease to Badshah's atheism. However, would they be able to explain why thousands and thousands of believers were also suffering from cancer? What sort of a divine justice is this?

Such unresolved questions flooded his mind whenever Badshah was at rest.

'Avik Roy,'—a middle-aged lady came out of the radiation room and announced the name. Sanjay and Mili took Badshah outside the waiting room and kept walking along the left side. After taking ten-twelve steps they crossed a swing door and found a sloping path. It took them further down to a small, flat space. There were two rectangular rooms on both sides of that flat space. Four technicians sat there with computers. They administered the radiation while the computer ascertained the required quantity in each case.

They sent Badshah to the room on the right side. By pushing a door in that room one can enter a dimly lit alley. A little ahead lay the actual area of radiation. Taking off their shoes, Badshah and Sanjay went inside that dark alley. Badshah was placed on a narrow bed. A belt, attached to the bed, held him in position. After a few seconds that electrically operated bed started to move upwards. Before that, they put a net-like mask on Badshah. At that moment, Sanjay had to vacate the space. The technician and another staff followed him out. Nobody was allowed to remain there during the process of radiation. This is done to ensure that no harm is caused by the radioactive rays.

Nearly seven minutes had passed before Badshah emerged outside. There was no visible sign of alarm or anguish on his face. Sitting on a stool, he put on the shoes. They were to go back in the same direction towards the swing door. The sloping path became uphill as they were returning, but dragging his right foot, Badshah slowly negotiated the path. He did not take the help of Sanjay's extended arm. Instead Badshah used his own left hand to support himself against the wall and kept moving up in that manner.

A card, with the reporting time of ten-thirty written on it, was given to them from the radiation centre. Every card thus issued bears different timings for the convenience of the crowd. As the number of machines was four, only four patients were provided the same timing. After reporting at ten-thirty, the technician selected a time within the duration of one and a half hour and informed the attendant of the patient. Accordingly, a specific dose of chemo-medicine was given to the patient. Usually during the course of radiation such doses were administered 'orally'. The same process was followed for Badshah. Every week, a five-day schedule, leaving aside the Saturdays and Sundays, was maintained for the completion of thirty-three radiation sittings. Chemo, however, had to be taken regularly. The TMH outdoor remained closed on Saturdays and Sundays. On those two days, chemo doses were taken at home.

On Saturdays and Sundays, they could relax a little. On weekdays they had to follow a routine of waking up early, getting ready in a hurry after a quick breakfast, and reaching TMH by Rintu's car in time. The weekends allowed that welcome respite.

Badshah also felt relieved on those two days. First, it was a welcome from the radiation schedule. Second the stress accumulated throughout the day was absent. Third he could spend time with Saswata and Soumya. The seventeen-year-old Soumya was Rintu's daughter. Rintu's wife was non-Bengali and also the siblings preferred Hindi as their means of communication with Badshah. Soumya was tireless in providing Badshah with the much-needed psychological support. She kept on explaining to Badshah that the disease was curable.

Every day, on their return from TMH, Saswata asked the customary question: 'How was the day?'

Generally, it was Sanjay who replied: 'Oh! It was all right. Today Badshah bhaiya took the lift and went alone. We climbed the stairs.'

This whetted Saswata's curiosity: 'That's great! This means he is steadily growing in confidence.'

Sanjay agreed. 'Right you are. It will increase gradually.'

The regular visits did boost up Badshah's confidence. That day, he went all by himself, boarding the lift to the underground radiation centre. The lift was too cramped for space. So Sanjay and Mili climbed down the stairs.

Saswata chatted to his heart's content with Badshah on Saturday-Sundays. He was well aware of Badshah's passion for football. Naturally, the game enjoyed quality time and presence in their discussion. English Premier League, La Liga, Messi and Ronaldo; the conversation was all-encompassing. Saswata supported Manchester United while Badshah rooted for Arsenal. However, the brothers were in consensus about their favourite player: for them it was not Lionel Messi but Christiano Ronaldo. Likewise, Sanjay and Rintu favoured Messi.

During their Mumbai sojourn, the discussions and debates about football were thoroughly enjoyed by Badshah. Neither the disease nor the suffering could bother him, when he talked about football. Saswata intermittently played with a football inside their hall room. One day, unable to restrain his excitement, Badshah started to play with his brother. Sanjay, Mili, Rintu and even Saswata were taken aback by his enthusiasm. Saswata said, 'Badshah bhaiya, you are also playing! Aren't you feeling tired?'

Though he was breathing heavily, Badshah replied, 'Who cares about tiredness? I can play the whole day long.'

Such was Badshah, the football fanatic. He was ever ready to do anything for football.

Besides Saswata, he also spent time with Soumya. Rintu's apartment was spread over a large area, encircled by a boundary wall. A path ran beside the wall where, most evenings, Soumya walked with Badshah. As his right foot got stiff, Badshah used to walk slowly. An attentive Soumya also adjusted her pace accordingly. Every day, after Badshah's physiotherapy sessions were done with and her academic activities were completed, Soumya had a chit-chat with Badshah.

Badshah endured a lot of pain and misery during those days. However, there were some bright spots that lifted his spirit. Nearly two months passed away and 15 July announced itself. It was Badshah's birthday. Everyone was determined to celebrate the day in a grand way. Monica and the other friends nearby were invited. Rohan, Ruben, Krittika, Roger and his betrothed, Monica, all arrived in Mumbai for the party. An enterprising Saswata, with the assistance of Soumya, gracefully decorated the hall for the occasion. Mili took the onus of cooking a plethora of items while Sanjay ordered for the home delivery of butter chicken and ice-cream.

Badshah was on cloud nine that day. His friends arrived in the evening. Monica reached Mumbai from Bangalore in the morning and went to Krittika's flat. She and Krittika came together to Rintu's place around five. Rohan and Ruben entered a little later. Ruben was the elder brother of Rohan and very fond of Badshah. Working in Mumbai then, Ruben had a single-room flat at Andheri. Roger and Badshah were college-mates in Delhi. Roger had also brought his fiancee from Pune for the special occasion.

It was a gala party where everyone tried their best to maintain the facade that all was well with Badshah. They gathered the details about the ongoing treatment at TMH from Sanjay, but maintained a straight face in front of Badshah. Everyone returned to their place quite late at night after a sumptuous dinner.

The radiation course ended on 18 July. Two days later, Dr Rahul met them at the outdoor and said, 'The MRI will not be done immediately. You can return to Jamshedpur. Avik will come for MRI again on 5 September. Meanwhile, continue the chemo dose as prescribed.'

It was time to return home. For Mili and Sanjay it was a great relief! They had left home on 3 May. Badshah's illness and the consequent diagnosis of the deadly disease had caused a huge turbulence in their lives. There was no further information from her school where Mili had submitted a leave application. She was in touch with her colleagues, exchanging news about Badshah, but could not contact the authorities. In spite of everything, Mili was happy to bring Badshah back to his home. Sanjay felt the same way, though he too had no clue about his coaching institute.

Badshah's joy knew no bounds. Memories of Bangalore indeed crossed his mind fleetingly, but it was a hugely comforting feeling to return to Jamshedpur with his parents again.

13

IN HIS CITY

•••

On 24 July, Sanjay, Mili, and Badshah boarded the flight from Mumbai and touched down at Ranchi around two in the afternoon. Badshah had recovered well enough and his right hand and leg had retrieved a little bit of mobility. However, the complete restoration to his former self was still a long and arduous journey. Regular sessions of physiotherapy that had started in Mumbai, would continue for a few more months.

They hired a cab and set out for Jamshedpur. The three-hour journey ended at around five o' clock in the evening, when they reached the Kadma syndicate colony. Homecoming has a spiritual bonding of everything around the place; the city, the streets, and even each tree appear so endearing and personal.

Sanjay and Mili were overjoyed to bring their son home. Badshah was also happy to return to his familiar surroundings. Moreover, he was meeting Thampu after a prolonged illness-induced hiatus. both Ruhi and Badshah called their grandmother Thampu. Thampu herself was bedridden for three years, afflicted with several ailments. Severe neurological and cardiac problems apart, of late she had also suffered a haemorrhage and cerebral stroke. Thampu had heard about her grandson's disease and became very worried. Her sensitivity and emotional intelligence were still very -sharp but Thampu's power of expression had got impaired.

Both the grandmother and her grandson could scarcely restrain themselves when they met each other. Badshah patted Thampu's cheeks and said:

'How are you, Thampu?'

He noticed that she had degenerated considerably. Badshah tried his best to conceal his discomfiture from Thampu.

However, Thampu had by then noticed Badshah's bald head. She also perceived that her grandson's right hand and leg were unusually stiff. Though she could not understand the effects of chemotherapy, the glittering corners of Thampu's eyes revealed that she knew for sure that Badshah was suffering from a severe illness. She had lost the ability to weep due to her affliction. Her hands motioned Badshah to come close. Thampu rubbed her cheeks against Badshah's and he used his left hand to embrace her warmly.

After two days, visitors started to arrive. The residents of the Syndicate colony came to meet Badshah. All of them brought different fruits and a beaming Badshah chatted long with his neighbours. Within a few days, the search for a reliable physiotherapist was launched. Sourav, Badshah's friend from schooldays, gave them the information about Gautam Bharati. His chamber was at Sakchi, near the Dhalbhumgarh Club. Badshah was duly taken there. Perusing the reports, Dr Bharati said:

'We will try our best to improve Avik's condition. We have done similar cases in the past. You can stay assured of our service.'

It was decided that Badshah would not attend his chamber. Instead, Dr Bharati would send his staff for physiotherapy sessions at home.

Another centre at Sakchi was consulted. Similar arrangements were made. Thus, each day two experts supervised the physiotherapy sessions and Badshah made a serious effort to regain fitness. Mili always remained by her son's side. She inspired him continuously and discussed a lot of things with her son. Badshah, too, poured his heart out. He talked about his office, his days in Bangalore, and his friends; he even spoke a lot about Monica.

Mili never insisted on knowing more. Rather it was Badshah who kept on talking to her about how Monica had lost her mother in childhood, about her nurture at her grandmother's place, how she struggled to continue her studies. Badshah also told his mother how he got acquainted with Monica at a tutorial close to their house.

Mili was always aware of Badshah's magnanimous nature. These heartfelt conversations only served to strengthen her admiration. After Badshah grew into an adult, both mother and son had never found an opportunity to spend so much of time together. Thus, Mili and Badshah relished every moment of it. Badshah was also fond of singing. Often, he was found humming or rendering a song full throttle. The songs of Kabir Suman were his favourite. At times Badshah was heard singing aloud:

'Do not give up, oh friend,

Do not give up.

Rather, speak up, oh friend,

Speak up loudly.'

Badshah's schoolmates, college friends, and members of his football team in Jamshedpur, all came in numbers and also paid personal visits to their dear pal. Shocked at seeing his emaciated, bald figure, they could barely control their emotions. In the company of friends, Badshah too, barely managed to suppress the grief that kept on swelling within him.

Though both Badshah and his buddies could well see through the mutual pretence at normalization, in desperation, they remained stuck to the role. At their first meeting since Badshah was diagnosed with the fatal disease, his friends had tried to play down his concerns. They had vehemently said that the crisis would be short-lived and pretty soon everything would be all right.

In his effort to maintain composure, Badshah sat with his laptop and tried his hand at writing. Sometimes he surfed the internet, watched movies or played songs. He also rang up Monica at times or some other friends.

Sanjay and Mili kept a close check on Badshah's recovery, which as understood, would still require few more months. Meanwhile, Sanjay got in touch with Amit Sachdeva. Amit informed him that the company had sanctioned a further three months' leave for Badshah for the period of September to November. Sanjay also discussed some relevant matters with him. Amit expressed his satisfaction at Badshah's progress and wished him a speedy recovery on behalf of the entire staff. He then said to Sanjay:'Uncle, the office has decided to increase Avik's medical insurance coverage. Now it stands at four lakhs. We are furthering it by nine lakhs. You have to pay only a part of the premium. The rest would be arranged by the office.'

'This is indeed very good news,' said Sanjay, 'It will be a great help in Avik's treatment. Please tell me, how should I send the money?'

Amit said, 'I shall send you a message with the payment details.'

Sanjay thanked him profusely, before ending the call.

Badshah was listening keenly to the discussion. Sanjay told him everything. Afterwards, he sent the cheque to the insurance company. Thus, Badshah's medical insurance now added up to thirteen lakhs.

Badshah tried to give the amount as quickly as possible to his father. Neither did have a chequebook, nor was his right hand able enough for writing. Badshah was habituated to net banking via laptop. Before his illness, he used to send money to Sanjay's account to pay the EMI of his educational loan. Likewise, Badshah transferred the amount for this additional premium to his father's account.

One day, Badshah said to Mili, 'Ma, I am planning to leave Bangalore for good and come back to Jamshedpur. I will live with you here again.'

'But where will you get a job here?' Mili expressed her despair, 'Even the Tata Steel Corporation has stopped recruiting and are intent on downsizing.'

Badshah assured his mother by saying, 'There are so many private banks. I will surely get into one of them.'

Badshah's desire did not materialize eventually. However, Mili realized that for her son, as it was in his childhood, 'home' was still the most cherished place. Even after spending a lot of time in Delhi and Bangalore, those big cities attracted him little. Badshah was never swayed by lucrative career prospects. Instead, his heart longed to return to his roots, to be in his own city, always and forever.

14

NANAWATI

...

Their flight arrived in Mumbai after half-past ten at night. They waited for the crowd to thin out and also to avail a wheelchair for Badshah. A young man came straight inside the craft with the chair. Very carefully and adroitly, he carried the chair with Badshah seated on it, down the sloping stairs. Sanjay and Mili were relieved to find the descent smoothly negotiated without any injury or discomfort to their son. The frequent landing of flights had left their aircraft without a terminal, thereby increasing the anxiety of Badshah's parents. It was indeed a formidable challenge for Badshah to climb down the slope.

They waited near belt number three, as announced within the flight itself, to collect the luggage. After the luggage was gathered, they came outside where Rintu was waiting for them. Rintu was visibly shocked to see Badshah's eroded appearance.

With his countenance displaying obvious signs of fatigue and agony, Badshah said in a feeble voice, 'How are you, Chhotka?'

'I am fine, but how did your health worsen so quickly? We met only few days back and you looked much improved then!'

'Within days of your return, the headache escalated along with bouts of vomiting. Uncle, for a brief period of time the suffering was relentless.'

Without extending the conversation further, Rintu said, 'Let us drive straight to Nanawati. The ambulance is waiting.'

An ambulance stood near them. Along with the driver and a para-medical employee, the ambulance also had a doctor. Badshah was lifted on a stretcher and placed inside the vehicle. Sanjay and Mili sat beside him. Rintu sat between the driver and the employee.

As the ambulance took start, the doctor, a lady around thirty years old, requested Sanjay to provide the case-history of Badshah. Sanjay gave her a concise account from the beginning. Badshah, lying with his eyes closed, showed no interest in the narrative.

Mili sat stooping to keep a hand on Badshah. The ambulance gathered speed and raced through the Mumbai eastern bypass towards Nanawati Hospital.

It took forty minutes to reach Nanawati. Badshah was taken to the emergency department. After being briefed about the case and completing some routine check-up, the doctors present there suggested an MRI test to be done preferably by that night.

It was half past midnight. To Sanjay and Mili, an MRI at such an odd hour seemed an impossible idea. However, in Mumbai, that too was possible. Most of the hospitals are equipped with such arrangements. Rintu said, 'It has to be done by tonight. Then the treatment will accordingly start from tomorrow. Such facilities are available here.'

He requested Sanjay and Mili to return to Lokhandwala, but Sanjay decided to stay. He knew that without knowing the MRI report they would remain restless.

Then Rintu said, 'Well, at least go and eat something from the canteen.'

Sanjay asked Rintu, 'Did you manage to eat?'

'Yes, I did,' Rintu said, 'You have barely eaten anything the entire day. Please have something.'

Ideally, they were supposed to be famished. However, the gnawing concern about Badshah had effaced the appetite.

The canteen was small and narrow. Yet it remained open at night to cater to the patients, their relatives and friends, doctors, nurses, para-medical staff and other hospital staff. The place was always buzzing with people. Sanjay and Mili ate a little bit and returned quickly.

The nightlife of Mumbai is famous for its enchantment and splendour. The exotic appeal of the night here beggars description. Indeed, they are fabulously fortunate, who can savour the heady buffet laid out by the night unflinchingly. How easily it casts a magical veil over all sorrow, desperation, tears, torture and grief! In his previous visits to Mumbai, Sanjay had never realized the sordid reality of the famed Mumbai night, expertly concealed by the mind-boggling razzmatazz.

However, the facade was blown away by Badshah's predicament and the city of dreams, with warts and all lay exposed to Sanjay. For him, it was like a netherworld intent on scaring the wits out of him.

They reached Nanawati before ten in the morning. Around six hours of rest and early breakfast had been quite refreshing.

They met Rintu who took them to the waiting hall. There he informed Sanjay and Mili about the doctor's opinion regarding the MRI report. Dr. Piyush Patil, nearing forty or so, was the topmost oncologist at Nanawati Hospital. According to Dr Patil, fluid had formed within Badshah's brain and spread well into the spinal cord. Consequently, the malignancy might have made inroads into the spine, the confirmation of which required a biopsy. The situation had obviously become grimmer.

Sanjay had never anticipated such abysmal deterioration. He knew nausea and headache were tell-tale symptoms of neurological ailment. Many years ago, in 1988, his mother had suffered a brain hemorrhage. A college of physicians of Patna, working in unison, saved her life. It was almost a miracle. Sanjay's mother also showed the same symptoms of vomiting and headache.

Badshah too experienced similar discomfort. It started during Bappa's wedding in Kolkata, especially as he vomited a lot on the day of the boubhat ceremony. They were staying at the clubhouse and on that day only Rajveer was there with Badshah. It was Rajveer who rang up and conveyed the news. Mili returned as fast as possible from the place of reception. Seeing her son considerably enfeebled, Mili opted to stay back with Badshah.

Before that, Badshah had kitted up appropriately and attended the main occasion. He sat for a long stretch of time with others and enjoyed the proceedings. When he began to feel unwell a little later, Badshah felt it wise to return to the clubhouse. He then informed Rajveer who accompanied Badshah to the club-house.

Sanjay and Ruhi, after receiving Mili's call, also went back. Perhaps nobody else was aware of Badshah's sickness. They decided against informing everyone too, lest it would jeopardize the entire program.

Such was Badshah. Fighting the monumental battle for survival against such a dreaded ailment and enduring the chemo doses which had such terrible side-effects, Badshah was steadfast in his decision to attend his elder cousin's wedding in Kolkata. It was a moving testimony of his indefatigable spirit. The majority, understandably, withdraws into an impregnable shell of apprehension, once they hear the name of cancer. The mere knowledge of being afflicted with cancer wreaks havoc in their lives. Swept into the vortex of dejection, they lose all zest for life and the will to lead a normal life again.

But Badshah was made of sterner stuff. Before the surgery in Bangalore, he became conscious of the fact that his illness was something serious. Post-surgery, when his right hand and leg got impaired, Badshah accepted the challenge and went through the physiotherapy sessions with exemplary enthusiasm. His sincere endeavour towards retrieving his fitness was a lesson for everyone around him.

Badshah had done physiotherapy sessions with a lot of people. After a period of frantic searching which included enquiry at the Columbia Asia in Bangalore to TMH in Mumbai and some other prominent places, it was Rintu who came across a young lady at an orthopedic centre at Lokhandwala. Her name was Chetna. She had completed a major course on the subject and was an accomplished physiotherapist. She helped Badshah with the sessions for almost two months. Even Chetna was highly impressed with Badshah's eagerness to get back in shape. Likewise, other physiotherapists also expressed their glowing admiration for his untiring struggle to reclaim fitness. Badshah had indeed displayed such remarkable attitude at different stages of his treatment. Whether it was radiation or chemo, MRI or something related, Badshah's grit was always conspicuous.

Apart from the touching anecdotes of his spectacular battle against cancer, there were numerous instances of Badshah's vibrant personality. At office, after completing his own duties, he willingly helped others or teamed up to finish their work. Badshah's attractive appearance and amicable nature made him popular among his colleagues. It was during his treatment at Columbia Asia in Bangalore, that Sanjay and others heard such rousing tales of appreciation about Badshah's professional prowess.

Everyone was well aware of the heartfelt affection which Badshah had for his friends. Since his schooldays, he used to choose his friends carefully and maintained a profound amity with them. Badshah disliked making friends merely to gossip or to kill the time. He wanted to learn more about man and understand the cause of his actions. He was warmly empathetic about people. School buddies, playmates, neighbourhood acquaintances and even his college and MBA batch-mates; Badshah was free and frank with each of them. He always shared their joys and sorrows and the friends reciprocated his feelings appropriately. They enjoyed an amazing comfort level with Badshah.

Generally, people remain conscious about their surroundings following either of the two perspectives; firstly, to view everything around by positioning oneself at the centre. Opinions are based on this perception and actions are taken likewise. The second manner was to treat oneself as a part of the greater picture. This develops an objective perception about the general characteristics and inconsistencies, thereby helping an individual to chart his plans or direct his initiatives. Obviously, this increases the responsibilities and one can no longer lead a self-absorbed existence. Neither can the person practice neutrality nor maintain indifference. One has to go beyond the personal interests to serve the greater cause. It creates a peculiar desire and drives people towards fulfilling it.

Badshah belonged to this second group. He wanted to live with and for the people. Unfettered by his joy or grief, benefits or discomfort, he always stood for the greater good and flexed himself according to the demands of the situation. Even the fatal malady failed to put a dent in his attitude towards life. Thus, amidst the chemo treatment, Badshah was resolute enough to attend his cousin's marriage ceremony in Kolkata. For that he bravely endured the bus ride from Jamshedpur to Kolkata. Notwithstanding the unnerving side-effects of the chemo doses and the strain of physiotherapy, Badshah reached the wedding simply by putting mind over matter. His parents were there for support. His elder sister and brother-in-law, too, flew in from Delhi. Still, very few can throw the gauntlet at the face of seemingly insurmountable obstacles like Badshah who defied all hurdles to reach the family function. Admittedly it was a gala occasion to meet the near and the dear ones, but only individuals like Badshah can wage even their lives for that.

As the ceremony rolled on, Badshah's illness got aggravated. Persistent headache and vomiting severely sapped his strength. Only a couple of days ago, Badshah, on the day of the wedding, was all smiles, enjoying the bus-ride to Kasba Rathtala from Maheshtala. Despite his fragile health, he tried to participate actively with others in the chores related to the auspicious event. Two days later, Badshah had to leave the boubhat mid-way. He barely ate that night. Badshah grew increasingly pensive and tight-lipped. He hardly communicated barring expressing his concern to Kakimoni about the irksome condition of the wedding party bus which they were to board again for the return journey to Jamshedpur. The vehicle was quite unsuitable for a long trip. Seats were uncomfortable enough. The sub-standard backrest forced everyone to sit in an erect posture. However, that was a journey of two hours whereas Kolkata to Jamshedpur would take eight to nine hours. Badshah was justifiably alarmed. He said, 'Kakimoni, I will not be able to make the journey by bus.'

Sharmila did convey Badshah's concern to Partho and Sanjay also voiced the same doubt. Bappa, on hearing it, waved aside the apprehension claiming that Badshah would feel better in the company of others within the bus. Travelling separately in a car, according to Bappa, might cause trouble. Partho seconded Bappa's suggestion.

Thus Badshah had to endure the bus journey. He kept on throwing up all along. It was such a pitiable experience for all inside the bus! Later, the MRI report at Nanawati confirmed what excruciating agony Badshah had undergone during that period! Recurrence is an integral feature of this disease. This explains why it is so deadly. It was much later that they came to know about the incurable nature of grade 4 brain tumour. Survival rate is almost nil.

The headache was unrelenting. Rintu returned to Mumbai. Before leaving he consulted a doctor from TMH and was informed about a medicine to alleviate the headache.

The drug was duly administered but it failed to eradicate the pain. It became an off-and-on affair. Badshah accordingly felt relaxed in its absence and so did Sanjay and Mili. Whenever the torment recurred, Badshah endured it in silence. Lying down, he gently rubbed his head or pressed his right hand against the left side of his head.

Sanjay and Mili wanted to take Badshah to Mumbai as early as possible. However, certain arrangements had to be made and that would be time-consuming too. They agreed to ask Rintu to inform the physicians at TMH about the condition. Badshah's check-up was scheduled in next March and it was only December! But Badshah's predicament cried for immediate medical assistance.

Rintu suggested them to book flight tickets without delay. As was the trend, if you want to buy tickets for a nearer date, you have to pay a steep price. Bought on the day of the journey, the ticket price can rocket up hopelessly. Considerable difference in cost happens if the tickets are booked a few months before. The process required proficiency in online banking and Sanjay neither had the expertise nor the means to do so. He thought of taking the help of a travel agent, a process which would obviously exact extra money.

Suddenly he realized that Ruhi-Rajveer could easily spare him the trouble. No sooner did he contact them than the tickets were made. At first, they booked the tickets for 31 December. But Rintu rang up and told them to come at an earlier date. It was 24 December and another week's delay would be ill advised. Badshah's headache was steadily worsening.

Rajveer-Ruhi kept on searching afresh for vacancies. There were plenty of flights for Mumbai from Kolkata but how could Badshah tolerate the stress of such a detour? From home to station, there to Howrah—in itself a four-hour journey and then to Dumdum airport, another one and a half hours! All together it would be nearly a seven-hour ordeal for Badshah! Rather, it was wiser to opt for Ranchi in an AC cab. It would take them two and a half hours to reach the airport. Though flights to Mumbai were fewer from Ranchi, after much deliberation, they agreed to avail that alternative. From Delhi, Rajveer booked the tickets. On 29 December, around four in the afternoon, they would board the Indigo flight. By seven in the evening, they would reach Mumbai.

Sitting at the waiting-hall of Nanawati hospital, Mili mused on the numerous impediments they had to overcome to bring Badshah to Mumbai. High hopes brought them here as lots of reassuring tales were heard about Nanawati. Celebrities and stalwarts flocked there in numbers to receive treatment. Redoubtable doctors served this institution. But Mili could hardly believe what those eminent physicians had to say! According to them, Badshah had very little chance of surviving the dreaded disease!

Mili and Sanjay found such observation too heart-rending to accept. Badshah was in the ICU. Only one person was permitted to visit the patient. They had not met him for hours. Mili could not restrain herself any longer. Taking the twenty-four-hours pass card from Rintu, she rushed inside.

Seeing Mili, Badshah said, 'Where were you all this time? I suffered a lot. Where is Baba?'

'He is waiting outside. Here they allow only one.'

Then she asked, 'Where is it hurting the most?'

Badshah touched his head and said, 'Here.'

A sister came forward and enquired, 'Ma'am, are you Avik's mother?'

Mili answered, 'Yes.'

The sister said, 'Towards the morning, Avik suffered two seizure attacks. Have you seen his MRI report?'

'No,' said Mili, 'We have heard about it from Dr. Patil.'

The sister further informed, 'A neuro-physician, specially summoned for Avik, will arrive soon. Do meet the doctor after the examination of the patient is completed.'

As the conversation was going on, the neuro-physician Dr. Shah entered the ICU. He asked for the MRI report after checking Badshah. Mili noticed that Dr. Shah's face wore a solemn look as he perused the report. After some time, he asked the sister, 'Where are Avik's parents?'

The sister pointed at Mili and said, 'This is Avik's mother.'

Dr. Shah said, 'Where is his father? Call him too.'

The sister forwarded the instructions to Mili and informed the ICU gatekeeper to allow Sanjay inside. Immediately Sanjay came in.

Moving some distance away from the bed, Dr Shah started to speak, 'I am not sure whether you are in complete awareness about Avik's disease. Indeed, it is brain cancer but in his case, it is particularly grade 4. In medical terminology it is called GBM or GLIOBLASTOMA, being the rarest of the rare, it affects very few people. It is an absolutely dangerous disease. Actually, speaking it has no cure. Avik's days are numbered now. Please strengthen your minds for the inevitable.'

Everything suddenly went blank for Sanjay and Mili. Fighting for words, Sanjay said, 'Why doctor? A few months back Avik was recovering well. His speech and the movement of the limbs have become quite normal recently.'

Dr. Shah remained silent for a few moments and then looked up in all tenderness towards Sanjay, 'That's true. He had received the appropriate treatment and Avik responded considerably too. But recurrence is unavoidable in this case. If it sets in again, there is nothing left to be done. In Avik's case, the worst has happened. I am extremely sorry.'

Tears welled up in his eyes, Sanjay stood speechless. He lowered his gaze. Mili tried to press her aanchal against her eyes, in a futile attempt to choke the tears.

Dr Shah placed his right hand on Sanjay's shoulder and shook him lightly, 'Take care Mr. Roy. Be strong.'

'Sorry doctor,' Sanjay replied in a low voice. Suddenly his eyes fell on Badshah who was staring at them intently. Though he could not hear them, he was trying to comprehend. Certainly, the sight of a sobbing Mili did not escape his attention.

They had to face their son. Looking at Mili, Sanjay touched her shoulder and said, 'Be steady. Badshah has seen us.' Wiping her teary eyes, Mili tried to pull herself together. Few moments later, they came near Badshah's bed and saw he had turned to the other side. Badshah's eyes were firmly shut.

He did not let out any sign of overhearing Dr. Shah or the conversation that followed. He might have listened and understood that he was a hopeless case. Perhaps he did not want to reveal his devastated state to his much-distressed parents.

Or else, Badshah was still in the dark about the fast-approaching end. He might have guessed that the doctor was discussing his condition with his parents. It was pretty easy for him to assume that the conversation had serious content.

Mili rested her hand lightly on Badshah's forehead. Badshah did not open his eyes. She understood that it was likely her son had heard everything or else was trying to find solace in ignorance.

Had he given up? Had he made up his mind not to continue the lopsided struggle anymore? Had he accepted his fate?

Mili could well remember how animatedly Badshah used to sing his favourite Kabir Suman number, even few days before Bappa's marriage:

'Do not give up, oh friend,

Do not give up.

Rather, speak up, oh friend,

Speak up loudly.

For we will surely meet again,

To greet the morning with a new song.'

Often when Badshah sang full-throated, Mili and Sanjay stood outside his room and listened. They looked at each other while listening to their son's soul stirring rendition. After Badshah had finished, Mili was the first to enter the room and cuddle him. Allowing his emotions a bit of time to settle, Sanjay would make a late entry. On that day, with their dear son lying on the hospital bed, they eyed each other again and tried desperately to understand one another.

At that moment, Rintu called Sanjay outside. He said, 'The consultation with the doctors here is over. So, let us dash to the TMH with the MRI report. Let us hear out the experts there. I hope to meet Dr. Rahul in the OPD. He has been treating Badshah for such a long time.'

Sanjay quickly gathered the report and the two brothers rushed towards TMH. Mili remained at Nanawati with Badshah.

They took an auto to get down at the nearby station to board a train for Dadar. Though TMH was at Parel, but the closest station was Dadar. From there to again got into an auto plying on a share basis.

It was touching mid-day when they arrived at TMH. Neuro OPD was chock-a-block as usual. Rintu submitted Badshah's file and on enquiry he was intimated that Dr Rahul was present.

Dr Rahul's call came after a moderate period of anxious waiting. He promptly recognized Rintu as he had met the doctor several times since their first visit. Even when Badshah returned to Jamshedpur after a phase of treatment, Rintu came to Dr Rahul's chamber to exchange the necessary updates or to gather the required advice.

Meeting Rintu again, the doctor asked, 'How is Avik?'

Rintu replied, 'Some complications have surfaced recently. After ten days from taking the fourth round of 320 dose chemo, the headache and vomiting increased rapidly. Thus, his parents brought him to Mumbai on the 29th. As the flight arrived late, we decided to admit him for the night at Nanawati. It is quite close to the airport and as you are aware securing indoor admission here is rather tough.

Dr. Rahul nodded approvingly. Then he said, 'Well, did they conduct an MRI at Nanawati?'

'Yes doctor,' Rintu confirmed, 'This is the report.'

Dr. Rahul studied the report for a long stretch of time. He also discussed it with his assistants.

'The tumour has got reduced in size, which is good enough development. But it seems like fluid on the wall of the brain. If the malignancy has used this fluid to spread itself comprehensively, that will be very bad indeed. However, to reduce his unbearable headache, shunting has to be resorted to without further delay. Next we will do the biopsy to ascertain the extent of the malignancy.'

Dr. Rahul stopped to gather his breath. He had been speaking very fast.

Rintu said, 'Can the shunting be done at your hospital?'

Dr Rahul said, 'Yes, certainly, it can be arranged here. Nevertheless, take the opinion of the neurosurgeon. Possibly he is in his chamber now.'

'What is his name?' asked Ritu.

'Dr Venkat. He is an eminent surgeon.'

Rintu looked for Dr Venkat and found his room to be on the opposite side of Dr Rahul's chamber.

Rintu quickly submitted Badshah's file so that it could reach Dr Venkat beforehand.

There are some rules at TMH which are applicable for each and every patient. In every OPD the chambers are arranged in rows with a counter in the middle. The files are submitted at the counters. After the computer entries are done with, the files are sent to the respective chambers. The assistants or the junior doctors study the cases and forward them to the senior doctors with relevant comments. Then on a first-come-first-serve-basis the patients and their attendants are summoned inside. Following this procedure, the ever-increasing number of patients are effectively treated at the hospital. Though it is time consuming and a gruelling test of patience, such an enormous crowd can be attended to only in this manner.

When their turn came, they entered the chamber and met Dr Venkat and his assistant. Perusing the MRI report, the doctor said, 'The tumour has shrunk in size. But fluid has accumulated around the brain. Also, the fluid has possibly entered into the spine. The shunting has to done immediately, otherwise Avik's agony will increase by leaps and bounds."

Rintu asked, 'Will it be done here? I am making the enquiry because it is very difficult to get a bed here. Isn't it doctor?'

'You are right,' said Dr Venkat, 'After the shunting, a machine called programmable chip will be inserted inside his head. It is better if you can find a standard quality machine. An expensive and effective machine will be immensely beneficial in the extraction of fluid from the patient's brain. Consequently, the patient will suffer less. Such machines are not available at TMH. As the treatment here is low-cost, such highly priced machines are not generally kept in stock.'

Dr Venkat advised that it would be better if the shunting was proceeded at Kokilaben.

Sanjay and Rintu readily agreed. Money was not an issue. Badshah's office had substantially stood by their side. In the first year which meant 2016, his Mediclaim coverage was four lakh which was the same for every employee. However, during this year, as a special case, another extra coverage of nine lakh was added to the previous four. Apart from that, a hefty amount of ten lakh was given to them by Badshah's office as one-time financial assistance. So there was no monetary roadblock regarding Badshah's treatment.

As they came out of TMH, Rintu said, 'Kokilaben is an excellent hospital. I hope to get skilled surgeons for shunting there. The programmable device shall be there too. Come on, let us try out Kokilaben on the way back to Nanawati.'

Sanjay said, 'Wait, let us eat something first. Let us look for an eatery. You have also not eaten anything.'

Both of them had gone starving throughout the day. There were some humble food stalls around the TMH serving pao bhaji, toast-omelette, rice and dal. They ate toast and omelette from a small roadside shop. It was nearing three o' clock in the afternoon. Rintu gathered the information that the OPD at Kokilaben would open around half past four. Dr Rajan Shah, a reputed neuro surgeon would be available there.

Accordingly, Sanjay and Rintu set out for Kokilaben around half past three.

15

KOKILABEN

...

The Kokilaben Dhirubhai Ambani Hospital at CharBangla in Andheri West was an imposing seventeen-storied building. State of the art in every respect, the hospital was served by eminent physicians and highly trained nurses, well supported by efficient management and latest gadgets. The younger of the Ambani brothers, who set up this hospital, named it after their parents. Money flowed lavishly in its construction and standardization. Thus it was no wonder that it was one of the most prominent hospitals in Mumbai. From the hallowed filmstars of earlier era to the present crop of Bollywood big-shots, Kokilaben basks with the pride of providing treatment to the celebrities.

Sanjay halted at the entrance of the ultra-modern institution. A long queue was being studiously scanned by the intensive security system. The metal detector check-up followed by the manual scrutiny was mandatory for securing entry inside. Initially, this entry procedure appeared challenging, but as their visits became regular later, it fell in place. As it is said, everything that looks difficult at first, becomes surprisingly easy afterwards.

Rintu asked the security for the way to the OPD to meet a neurosurgeon. Unlike other places, cards or passes were not required for such meetings here. The OPD was in the second floor where they gathered the information that among the neurosurgeons on duty, the most experienced was Dr Rajan Shah.

Sanjay and Rintu decided to take the advice of Dr Shah. Badshah's case was undoubtedly grave and merited the consultation of the best. On depositing the requisite fee for appointment, within a short time, they were called inside his chamber.

Dr Shah's stout appearance was in contrast to his advanced years. He listened intently as Sanjay narrated the case history. Then he studied the MRI report thoroughly. After that Dr. Shah said, 'Yes, the tumour has become smaller in size but the regrowth, taking the form of fluid, has spread itself considerably. Shunting will obviously provide relief to the patient. If you wish you can bring him here. The sooner you can come, the better it will be for the patient.'

Rintu glanced at his watch; it was close to six. Would it be possible to shift Badshah so fast? It would be an uphill task. It would take another hour for them to reach Nanawati. It would be well beyond the time of discharge by the hospital. Rather, they had not yet responded to the hospital authorities who wanted to elaborate on their treatment plan with them.

Rintu said, 'We have at least got an idea about the line of action now. Shunting has to be done immediately. It is better to have it in done at Kokilaben. Dr Rajan Shah appeared reassuringly confident.'

Sanjay replied, 'Still, we have to consult the doctors at Nanawati. We will try to take Badshah to Kokilaben by tomorrow afternoon. The shunting can be done on the next day. Then we will contact TMH.'

Mumbai, at dusk, wears a glittering look. The smooth roads manifest a ceaseless flow of cars. Rows of bright lights adorn the streets appropriately. Admittedly, there are places where craters do play spoilsport while some streets are quite shabby and narrow. However, Mumbai, the city of glitz and glamour, with roads flooded with light and cars from Nariman Point to Worli-Churchgate-Choupatty indeed creates an ambiance of opulence, which is almost impossible to ignore. In contrast, the area around Dadar was rather congested and dingy. In his earlier visits, Sanjay too had profusely admired the wonder that is Mumbai. The seamier side which he had seen then did not stay in the mind for long.

Badshah's treatment and the associated worries had considerably dampened their spirits. This time, Mumbai also appeared different. Roads marred with potholes, garbage heaped here and there, local trains bursting at seams with commuters, pickpockets, and snatchers making merry; the famous Mumbai sparkle seemed conspicuously missing. Share-autos were hard to find and so were the public buses. In an emergency, one had to reserve an auto or taxi at a hopelessly high price.

The cost of living in Mumbai is higher than in other Indian cities. It is an immensely tough task to find or rent a shelter in the city of dreams. To live and maintain a decent living standard in Mumbai poses a stiff challenge. Yet the lure of the city is such that people who have arrived and spent a few days here, develop an unending love affair with Mumbai.

Sanjay and Rintu took an auto and reached Nanawati around eight in the evening. In between they had phoned Mili. Badshah was stable. Though there was no further seizure, he complained about headaches now and then.

Sanjay went straight to Badshah. He was full of questions and concerns regarding the whereabouts of his father. His mother informed him that Baba and Chotka had gone to TMH to consult with the doctors. Badshah himself felt assured about the place. For two months he had taken thirty-three radiations and forty-five chemo there. Though he was treated at the OPD yet Badshah felt a lot better after the treatment at TMH.

'Baba, what did the doctors say? Will this headache diminish?' asked Badshah.

Sanjay said, 'Yes son, it will go away. You require a small operation for that. It is called shunting. According to the advice of doctors at TMH, it is better to get the operation done at Kokilaben. Then we went to Kokilaben and had a discussion with the doctors. Tomorrow we will take you there.'

Badshah listened to his father quietly. He had reservations about Kokilaben Hospital. On their previous visit to Mumbai, Badshah was taken there for physiotherapy. It was a harrowing experience. After waiting for hours, they met a person who rushed through the drills and ended the session with inexplicable nonchalance. An utter lack of sincerity and professionalism left Badshah bitterly disappointed. Sanjay and Mili were also much dismayed at the matter.

That disconcerting memory obviously raised doubts. On the flip side though, the institution did redeem itself in their eyes by providing stellar service during an emergency. During their two-month-long stay in Mumbai, one-night Badshah suddenly experienced intense palpitation. He understandably became nervous. Sanjay, at that time, had returned to Jamshedpur to attend some pressing matters.

Without wasting time, Rintu took him to the emergency section at Kokilaben. Tests and analysis promptly followed. However, nothing alarming was detected. It was a panic attack triggered by his anxious frame of mind. That night the altruistic efforts of the doctors and the hospital staff were much appreciated by Badshah.

It was difficult to ascertain the level of mixed emotion that the mention of Kokilaben evoked within Badshah. Probably he felt a little at ease.

'Baba, tomorrow at what time shall we go there?' asked Badshah.

'Let me consult the doctors here. However, we will try to reach there as quickly as possible so that the shunting can be done by tomorrow.'

The reassuring words of his father seemed to soothe the worry of Badshah.

Later Mili told Sanjay that the treatment at Nanawati was causing much distress to Badshah. To alleviate his problems during urination, they tried to attach a catheter. However, they did not adopt the necessary measures before the insertion. Consequently, Badshah suffered a lot of pain. He screamed in unbearable agony. Mili tried to point out the problem. The indifferent staff however refused to acknowledge their mistake. Rather they admonished Badshah for wailing! So, an annoyed Badshah was happy to bid adieu to Nanawati.

Rintu, anxious about his nephew's disposition, at first asked Badshah about the headache. He heaved a sigh of relief after confirming from Mili that there was no attack of seizure in the meantime.

He said to Badshah, 'Tomorrow, after discharge, we are going straight to Kokilaben where the shunting will take place. Their infrastructure is absolutely first class and updated.'

Chotka's cheering words enlivened Badshah a lot.

Sanjay requested Rintu to return home. It was close to nine. Rintu had remained wide awake throughout the previous night, followed by the running around for the entire day. If the same routine got repeated tonight, an exhausted Rintu would surely fall ill.

Rintu was severely reluctant to return. Rather he wanted to send Sanjay and Mili to his home. However, they remained firm and Rintu had to relent. Before leaving, Rintu promised to return by nine-thirty in the morning.

At night, nobody was allowed inside the CCU. The relatives of the patients took shelter in a narrow corridor beside the CCU. With a few benches available, most of them had to stretch themselves on the floor. Helping Mili to recline on a bench, Sanjay sat near her feet.

Sleep evaded Sanjay's restless mind. It was crammed with vagrant reflections. Is there really no medicine that can cure Badshah? Throughout the world, the endeavour to find a wonder drug to conquer cancer has been going on for ages. Till date, umpteen scientific researches have bitten the dust and a colossal amount of money have all been a grand waste. Even today, this fatal disease wreaks havoc in the absence of any substantially satisfactory treatment.

Earlier Sanjay used to hear about cancer patients among his relatives, friends, or neighbours. Saddened by such news, he felt sorry for them. Beyond that, cancer bothered him little. With his own son fighting for survival against cancer and doctors confessing their limitations, Sanjay was flayed by ghastly thoughts. As the shadow of death steadily lengthened over his son, Sanjay's mind got increasingly blurred with bewilderment.

It was 1972-73. The father of Sanjay's dearest friend Pulu became a victim of blood cancer. There was no treatment for cancer in those days at Patna. His friend's father was frequently taken to Kolkata for plasma therapy. After an agonizing tug-of-war for two years, the elderly gentleman passed away. It was a shattering experience for Sanjay as he witnessed how Pulu's family almost crumbled in bereavement. It took them long enough to recover from the shock. During that period, Sanjay spent long hours at Pulu's house lending support and comfort to his closest friend.

The sleepless night at Nanawati allowed those dim memories to rejuvenate. Sanjay glanced at Mili whose fatigue was graced by slumber. At once Sanjay felt anxious about Badshah. Was he sleeping? Was the obstinate headache tormenting him too much? He felt a strong urge to check if all was well with Badshah. Sanjay went to the far side of the corridor towards the way to the CCU. He pushed a small door open and found another bigger door on the other end of a small rectangular passage. The gatekeeper, sitting on a stool was fast asleep. It was an hour past midnight.

Sanjay softly called, 'O Bhai!' There was no response. Then Sanjay put his hand lightly on the gateman's shoulder. It had the desired effect. Startled by the untimely alarm, he woke up and said, 'What happened?'

Sanjay allowed him to gather himself up. Then he said, 'My patient is in CCU. Bed number 7. He is my son.'

The man replied in a low voice, 'Well, so what?'

'If you don't mind, please go and check his condition,' requested Sanjay.

'What, now, so late in the night! Entry is prohibited now. In the morning, I'll check and inform you.'

The man closed his eyes again.

Sanjay pleaded, 'O brother, please check and tell me now. Just for once.'

The gatekeeper shook off the languidness and entered the CCU. About ten minutes later he returned.

'Now he is fine. Earlier he complained of headache, but after taking the medicine, the patient has gone to sleep.'

Sanjay realized that Badshah's agony had been temporarily subdued by painkillers. Shunting was sorely needed. Further delay would only accelerate his misery.

A pensive Sanjay returned to the bench. Mili, like many others in that corridor, was in deep sleep. However, an individual who looked to be forty-five years, was wide awake. He asked in Hindi whether Sanjay had gone inside the CCU.

Sanjay said, 'No, I requested the gatekeeper to go inside and visit my patient.'

'What is your relation with the patient?'

'He is my son.'

'Your son!' the man sounded concerned. 'What is his problem?'

'Brain Cancer. That too a grade 4 stage.'

'Oh! Oh! Brain Cancer,' the listener's expression was a blend of shock and surprise.

Sanjay asked, 'What about you?'

He replied, 'My father has been admitted here with cardiac problem.'

'How old is he?'

'Seventy-two. He has been suffering from cardiac issues for a long time.'

'Do you live here, I mean, in Mumbai?'

The man said, 'Yes, in Mumbai. My grandfather came from Ahmedabad and settled here.'

Then he asked about Sanjay's home.

'We are from Jharkhand,' replied Sanjay. 'Are you familiar with the name?'

His sleepless partner immediately affirmed, 'Oh yes. I know about Jharkhand.' Then he tried to be more precise with his awareness, 'Dhoni comes from there.'

It was Sanjay's turn to nod and approve. The all-encompassing popularity of cricket in India is an undisputed truth. Cricket heroes are household names and Dhoni is one of the most revered in that pantheon of superstars. Dhoni, the swashbuckling batsman and maverick skipper, won the World Cup for the country in T-20 as well as in the ODI format. Furthermore, his brilliant leadership took India to the number one position in the Test cricket ranking. Dhoni, the megastar of the cricket crazy nation, has innumerable die-hard fans who take pride in their knowledge about their hero. So any mention of Jharkhand at once gets connected with MSD.

Sanjay said, 'We are from Jharkhand but not Ranchi. Our home is at Tata, I mean, Jamshedpur."

Taking a little time, the man said, 'Yes, it is the place from where the trucks made by Tata come.'

Sanjay confirmed his statement and added, 'Right you are. It is the home of Telco Company. The Tata trucks do roll out from there.'

The nocturnal chit-chat had brought the two anxious individuals closer. In between their conversation, the man observed Mili and asked, 'Is there anyone else accompanying your son apart from you and Madam?'

'We have brought him to Mumbai. But, my younger brother, who stays at Lokhandwala, is with us all along the course of treatment.'

'Your own brother, at Lokhandwala?'

'That's right. During my son's prolonged treatment, we used stay at his place.'

'It saved you from a lot of fuss as people coming here for treatment find it frustratingly difficult to arrange for a shelter.'

'Certainly,' said Sanjay.

The conversation went on meandering from family concerns to ubiquitous matters. It served as a soothing antidote to Sanjay's dolorous mind. Badshah's terrible malady had effaced all happiness from their lives. Living had become an insipid drill. In such a vapid existence, while spending a stress-filled night outside the CCU which housed their fatally ill son, this endearing conversation provided much succour to Sanjay.

Dawn was making its presence felt. Mili had awakened. She sat up and asked Sanjay, 'How is Badshah?'

Sanjay said, 'Two hours ago, on requesting, I was told that Badshah was sleeping.'

'Try once again, and find out how he is faring now.'

The CCU by then had resumed its plethora of activities. The gateman sat ramrod straight. Sanjay peeped through the narrow gap. Nurses were administering medicines to patients. Some were injecting the same through the drip while others were checking their blood pressure. He could not spot Badshah properly. He said to the gatekeeper, 'Please go and see how the patient in bed number seven is doing.'

The gatekeeper looked at Sanjay and recognized him. He replied, 'Shortly I shall bring you the news. Just wait.'

Little later, the gateman once again confirmed the bed number from Sanjay and went inside. Within five minutes he came outside and said, 'Please come in. The sister wants to meet you.'

Sanjay felt perturbed. He feared that Badshah's condition might have worsened. Taking off the shoes, Sanjay put on the slippers assigned for the CCU and pushed open the swing door.

He went to the sisters' desk where he informed them about the bed number and his relation with the patient.

The senior sister started to brief him, 'Initially he slept under the influence of the painkillers. But later he woke up and from then on started to suffer the headache again. In extreme discomfort sometimes he had tried to call his mother too.'

Sanjay said, 'Please allow me to see him for a few minutes.'

Badshah was lying with his eyes closed. As Sanjay touched his forehead, Badshah slowly pried them open. Misery and fatigue lay juxtaposed on his visage.

Sanjay tenderly asked, 'Baba, how do you feel?'

Badshah replied in a low voice, 'Headache. Where is Ma?'

'She is waiting outside. As nobody at night is allowed within the CCU, we spent the night in the waiting hall. I am sending your mother inside.'

He ran his hand affectionately over Badshah's head and face. Badshah shut his eyes again.

Sanjay took leave from the sister and went out of the room. He informed Mili about everything and requested her to go inside.

Badshah was much relieved to meet his mother. He told Mili that though at present the terrible headache had allowed him a little breathing space, it had been tormenting him almost the entire night.

Mili said, 'Today we will leave for Kokilaben. Baba and Chotka have made the necessary arrangements. The shunting will take place there.' Badshah had earlier heard the same from his father. He maintained a tired silence.

Mili noticed that Badshah had weakened considerably. Probably it was caused by the incessant headache. His health too, had alarmingly degenerated. Mili doubted whether her son's mental strength had been ebbing steadily. She wanted to discuss it with Sanjay. With a heavy heart and dewy eyes she left the CCU. Mili, the ever-affable soul, found her composure crumbling vehemently under such unprecedented duress. Since childhood, though engrossed in studies and dancing, the ever-smiling Mili was always an animated individual. Indeed, her father's untimely demise dealt a devastating blow to her jovial nature. It imposed a stunned state of denial from everything she held dear. Thereafter, with her mother and elder brother for company, began the defiant struggle to survive the bereavement. At times a single day seemed like an era. Mili did receive the generous support of their relatives and friends. Still nothing could retrieve the vivacious little world of hers that had been annihilated with the passing away of her dear father. However, with Mili's elder brother getting employed and she herself resuming her academic pursuits, things started to look brighter with the passage of time. Happiness made a glorious return with a whirlwind of joyous happenings; she secured her B.A. degree, tied the nuptial knot with Sanjay and Ruhi and Badshah consequently arrived. Life seemed to bestow Mili a delightful melody and meaning once again. Living started to jig into an inviting routine of assurance and satisfaction.

Yet again disaster made fresh inroads into Mili's cosy cosmos as Badshah was diagnosed with cancer. Outside the CCU, in exasperation, she said to Sanjay, 'You have seen Badshah, haven't you? He is very unwell.' A disconcerted Sanjay tried to comfort his better half, 'Yes, I have seen his condition. We have to shift him as fast as possible to Kokilaben. By tomorrow, the shunting must be done.'

Rintu diligently arrived at nine o'clock. As doctors started to attend to their duties, Rintu began to enquire about the discharge procedure. The resident doctor informed him that bed number seven was supervised by Dr Patil. Hence, they met the same physician whom they had consulted about the MRI report the previous day.

Dr Patil was taken aback by their appeal for discharging Badshah. He said, 'Where do you want to shift the patient in this delicate condition? He requires targeted chemo which can obviously be arranged here.'

Rintu tried to reason, 'We agree with you doctor. But at first, the shunting has to be arranged to provide relief from that intense headache. We have been advised accordingly from TMH.'

On hearing the reference to TMH, Dr Patil responded with a few moments of silence.

Rintu, however, continued, 'All along, Avik was being treated there. Chemotherapy and Radiation; everything was done there. Till a couple of days before arriving in Mumbai, the TMH treatment guidelines were being meticulously followed by us."

Dr Patil agreed, 'Well, shunting is necessary. But only a neurosurgeon can take a final call on that. For that you have to consult with the in-charge of the CCU.'

They realized the situation perfectly. The professional world has a definite line of limitations for each employee. Nobody is willing to cross the line and face consequences. Rather each doctor here tries to work within that restriction, thereby serving the financial health of the hospital better than making appropriate decisions for the benefit of the patients. Every planning in the hospital is done with the ulterior motive of swelling the medical bill. Like the legendary archer Arjun, for the hospital management, profit is the bird's eye and attention must be riveted on it. Everything else can wait.

Surely there are exceptions like the Tata Memorial Hospital. It provides an exemplary service to cancer patients at an unimaginably low cost. The standard of treatment is top class and so is the selfless sincerity of the doctors and support staff. No wonder the institution enjoys nationwide fame with patients from all over the country rushing in overwhelming numbers to avail the care. TMH also attracts patients from neighbouring countries.

Rintu said to Dr Patil, 'Certainly, we will have a discussion with the CCU in charge. However, we have come to know that this hospital is presently without a neurosurgeon who is also a specialist in shunting. Thus, we are left with no other alternative but to seek the facility somewhere else.'

Dr Patil realized that the patient party had all the bases covered. Moreover, the patient's condition was very critical. The specialist neurosurgeon at Nanawati was on a long leave. He gave up, 'Well, please contact the discharge section. You will face no inconvenience on my part.'

Dr Siddiqui, a man in his early forties, was the CCU incharge. He listened attentively to Rintu's reporting and then commented, 'See, you are free totake away your patient. Avik is in urgent need of shunting and we lack the facility here at present. So his discharge procedure will be initiated according to your approval.'

Rintu replied, 'Please go ahead with the formalities. We are also informing the billing department about our decision.'

The billing section informed them that the final bill would be prepared after the receipt of the discharge report. Thereafter no further service would be provided. Payment could be done in either cash or card.

Returning to the CCU, they discovered that the discharge procedure had already started. Dr. Siddiqui had given the relevant instructions to the senior sister. The papers were being prepared accordingly. Dr Siddiqui also met Badshah who repeated the complaint regarding headache. Talking with Badshah, they strongly sensed that he was earnestly waiting to bid adieu to Nanawati. Mili, like the previous day, remained beside his bed.

Suddenly Sanjay was assailed by a doubt. Was the name of Kokilaben enlisted among the hospitals covered by the medical insurance company attached to Badshah's office? The very long list that contained the names of nearly all eminent private hospitals was surely not going to leave out Kokilaben. Still, it was wise to seek confirmation. The enlisted hospitals would provide completely cashless treatment. So, Sanjay decided to double-check with that magnanimous young man Amit Sachdeva. Amit, from the initial days of Badshah's affliction, had stood beside him offering assistance and sympathy. His respect for Sanjay and Mili was immense and his affection for Avik was heartfelt.

Amit answered Sanjay's call promptly. He promised to contact the HR department and ring back in a short while.

A cashless facility was not available at Nanawati. So, the debit card was swiped into service. Once again Sanjay was jolted with a fresh concern. It was on 31st December. The new year would commence from the next day and so would begin a new duration of Badshah's medical insurance. The coverage henceforth would be of nine lakh. With Amit pressing for the initiative, Badshah's office had, in exchange for a modest rise in premium amount, extended the coverage likewise from the existing four lakh.

Within half an hour Amit confirmed that Kokilaben was assuredly on the list. So the cashless facility was a certainty there. However, the new coverage would start from the first of January, 2017.

Sanjay discussed the matter with Rintu. As things were unfolding, the discharge procedure would run deep into the evening to get settled. If they could reach Kokilaben by nine, they would take Badshah straight to the emergency. Some diagnostic tests would surely follow. Immediately after midnight, the cashless admission would be availed.

The interim expenses, if any, had to be incurred personally and they were prepared for that.

Gathering all the papers related to discharge, an ambulance was called as soon as the final bill was paid. The ambulance fee of rupees one thousand was separately deposited at the counter. Nanawati Hospital provided a doctor, with medical law, to accompany Badshah to Kokilaben. Around half past eight, the ambulance commenced its journey.

16

NEW YEAR

...

A few minutes after nine, the ambulance arrived in front of the emergency department at Kokilaben Hospital. Though the nomenclature 'emergency' exudes gravity, in practice the department is usually steered by junior doctors. Thus, they consumed a lot of time straining to understand Badshah's problem. There was neither a neurosurgeon nor an oncologist in the emergency. Glioblastoma was too esoteric a proposition for the neophytes present there.

Sensing their predicament, Sanjay dropped the name of Dr. Rajan Shah and also elaborated on his advice regarding shunting. It had the desired effect. The junior doctors at once perceived the gravity of the case and remained contented with some routine clinical examination.

Badshah felt somewhat at ease since their arrival at Kokilaben. He had desperately wanted to get out of Nanawati. Moreover, he took heart from the superior infrastructure at Kokilaben. After the preliminary check-up, Badshah engaged himself in a frugal conversation with his parents and uncle. He wanted to know about the location of the hospital. On being informed, Badshah said, 'Then it is not far from Chotka's house. When will I go there?'

Mili soothed his frayed mind, 'My dear son, just be patient for a few days more. Let the shunting happen tomorrow. Then you shall require two to four days to recover. After that, we will certainly return to Chotka's flat.'

Badshah calmed down. A little later he said, 'Ma, I want to have some tea. Is it possible now?'

Sanjay asked for the permission of the attending doctors. A young physician readily responded, 'Oh, why not! I'll send someone to fetch tea. Avik, do you need biscuits?'

Badshah nodded.

Tea and biscuits were brought within fifteen minutes. Badshah sat up on his bed. While sipping tea, he also indulged in small talk with Mili. The excruciating headache had subsided comprehensively. His mother also was very relieved to find Badshah in a better state.

Suddenly Sanjay realized that midnight was only half an hour away. He was due for a visit to the admission counter.

Rintu said, 'Don't worry. I'll stay here.'

Taking the identity card of Badshah's office along with the card given by the Mediclaim company, Sanjay went to the admission counter.

Entering the hospital by the main entrance, one can see the emergency straight in front. There is also a platform which can be ascended using stairs on both sides. Beside that lies the rounded way for the movement of the stretchers. The path looked like a semi-circle. A huge glass door was positioned behind it. On the other side of that door was the waiting hall. There were several counters on one side of that hall. The admission procedure was conducted from one of those counters.

A smart young man of twenty-seven years or so was attending the visitors. Sanjay introduced himself and presented Badshah's case to him. He further requested to proceed with the admission formalities after midnight. The new medical insurance would come into effect only from 2017. Meanwhile, the policy made in 2016 had become exhausted. The sprightly youth, whose name was Amir, took some time to warm up to the matter. He said, 'I understand. You have to wait for another ten minutes to activate your new policy which will start from 1st January 2017.' Sanjay glanced at his watch and said, 'I am ready to wait for ten minutes. Please start the procedure after that.'

Amir replied, 'But you have to pay for the expenses incurred before midnight separately.'

Sanjay said, 'Obviously.'

No sooner did the clock strike twelve than Amir stretched his hand towards Sanjay and greeted him, 'Happy New Year Uncle!'

In a reflex action, Sanjay extended his hand, but he repeated the words vacantly. His mind could not comply with the spirit of gaiety associated with year ending. Every year, they do participate in the festive mood of ringing in the new year. After midnight, countless times, the 'happy new year' greeting is received and expressed. Life however got drastically transformed with the onset of their son's morbidity. They had to leave home and pursue his treatment in Mumbai. Badshah was worsening gradually. A terrible headache was wilting him alarmingly. The MRI report had been most discouraging. Under such strenuous conditions, the expression 'happy new year' felt raucous and rancid.

Yet the show must go on. Life force will provoke one to fall in line and follow the flow. Sanjay's weary eyes fell on the world on the other side of the big glass door. The entire Charbangla was flooded with festive lights. An incessant procession of cars provided a boisterous complement to the gala spirit. As far as he could see, the shops were all open, merrily defying the nocturnal routine. The festive crowd swarmed everywhere in a bid to welcome the new year. It was that time of the year when people studiously believe that happiness increases manifold times through sharing.

Sanjay reminded himself that he was in Mumbai, the city of dreams, which he had fervently wished to visit since his childhood. The city where the mesmerizing histrionics of Dilip Kumar, and Raj Kapoor, the lilting melodies like, Mera Joota Hai Japani… concocted a heady brew of fancy and frenzy; there stood a hapless

father on a New Year's Eve at a counter of the emergency department of a hospital. He was striving hard to secure admission for his son who was suffering from brain cancer. Fluid had formed within his brain, causing him unspeakable agony.

Amir perhaps sensed the lack of warmth in Sanjay's handshake. He became laconic in speech and completed the formal requirements. Then he requested Sanjay to deposit some money. After deducting the requisite amount for 31 December, the remainder would be adjusted with the next bill.

Sanjay said, 'Will forty thousand be sufficient?'

Amir replied, 'Surely.'

Sanjay swiped the debit card and deposited the amount.

Returning to the emergency, Sanjay saw that preparations for shifting Badshah to the CCU had begun.

He was admitted to CCU number 3 on the second floor. The arrangements were much to their liking. The number of doctors and nurses was slightly more in proportion to the patients. It was also substantially equipped with the necessary devices. Badshah was allotted bed number nine. Nobody was allowed to be with the patient except during the visiting hours. Notwithstanding Badshah's reluctance to let go of his mother, after some time, Sanjay, Mili, and Rintu had to leave the CCU.

Sending Rintu home, Sanjay and Mili stayed back. At Kokilaben, the patient party is provided with comfortable resting facilities. On the fifth floor, cots are laid like berths within a train compartment, where they can rest comfortably. At a little distance away stands a toilet.

On the first morning of January, they got up early, drank a cup of coffee each from the adjoining CCD, and arrived in front of CCU 3. The security refused to let them enter inside. On request, he went inside and brought them the news that Badshah was sleeping. The hospital seemed to be manned by very few staff that morning. Attendance was visibly poor. Even those who had reported for work appeared to be preoccupied by a festal mood.

Over the years, Sanjay had noticed that the advent of a new year creates a unique ambience within the country which is perfectly in harmony with the pluralistic spirit of India. Casting aside all identity issues, through the mutual exchange of greetings and gifts, a culture of synthesis is formed. Many fail to perceive it, but Sanjay could emphatically sense the widespread influence of capitalism at work. Even the otherwise god-fearing people have also jumped onto the bandwagon of the English New Year celebration. From small areas in the countryside to clubs here and there, programs and parties are a must to welcome the new year. If not the villages, the small towns have become happily habituated with this merriment. It has become an integral part of their lifestyle. On the first day of January or rather from the dying minutes of the thirty-first of December itself, the cries of 'happy new year' intensifies into an overwhelming cacophony. Wishes are abundantly exchanged via phone calls or messages and even through personal meetings. However, this does result in a situation where the warmth in the greetings often gets replaced by a mindless indulgence in ritualistic observance.

Sanjay has tried to understand the craze behind this superficiality. He has reasoned that life now is encumbered with a plethora of woes. This has comprehensively sucked out the joy of living. Thus, staggering at the moribund, life attempts to regale itself in vain with observance and celebration. Any excuse, be it a cricket match Durga Puja or the new year, provides a cause for ostentatious enjoyment. The observance has thus become synonymous with living. The triumph of capitalism precisely lies here. The mushrooming of celebration ensures rapid boom in the market. Products of different companies fly off the shelves in a hurry. People do not think twice in deferring essential expenditures to allocate money for various events that lure them into a shopping spree.

'Happy new year,' the junior doctor, with whom they got acquainted the previous night in front of Badshah's bed, had extended his hand.

'Same to you,' Sanjay, though lost in thoughts and a little bemused, reciprocated the greeting. The doctor was indeed a very young man whose face was lit with a tinge of joviality.

Sanjay asked, 'Is Dr Shah coming?'

'Certainly, Sir,' the smiling face responded.

'We need to talk to him about Avik.'

'Sir, please wait for some time. Surely you can have a discussion with him. He will be here by nine.'

Sanjay glanced at his watch. It was a few minutes past eight. He thought of sending Mili back to Rintu's flat.

Rintu's residence was quite close to the hospital. Autos were available. The movie tower at Yamuna Nagar in Lokhandwala, was merely two-three kilometers from the hospital. Mili could cover the distance easily by herself. Reaching there, she could send Rintu here as early as possible. It would be convenient if Rintu remained present during the discussion with the doctor.

Mili, however, disagreed. She said, 'Rintu will obviously reach by nine. Then I will leave.'

Sanjay said, 'Let us go downstairs to the canteen and eat something. I'm feeling very hungry.'

The canteen was spacious and well maintained. Depositing money for two plates of dosa and two cups of tea, they sat at a table.

They had barely completed the dosa and intended to take the tea, when the phone rang. It was Rintu.

'Where are you two?'

'Come to the canteen. We're there.'

Within five minutes, Rintu joined them. He refused to take anything except tea. The plan was made to meet Dr Rajan Shah in the morning itself. First to ensure the shunting, considering it was first January. Second, an estimate for shunting had be taken and accordingly, a discussion had to be arranged with the TPA for the medical insurance. TPA stands for Third Party Administrator. It is their responsibility to sanction the money for the insured patient from the insurance company. In Badshah's case, once the company approved the amount, the billing department of the hospital would give clearance and the shunting could be proceeded with.

Rintu wanted to verify whether the TPA office in Bangalore was open for the day. If it *was* open, they could go on with the task of seeking the necessary sanction from the insurance company. Badshah was in acute need of shunting, but they had no idea that the first day of January, in itself, could be the source of such an insurmountable impediment. It was an inexplicably frustrating experience!

Sending Mili home, Sanjay and Rintu went to the CCU to meet Dr Shah.

It was already nine and the doctor had arrived. The security at first denied them entry but let them go when he was informed about the purpose of their visit. Dr Shah himself came forward and greeted them. He said, 'I have seen Avik. He is stable otherwise. But the shunting will pose a problem for today. The cost will be almost one and a half times more than usual. Today being a holiday, the expenditure will understandably escalate.'

Sanjay said, 'See, the money is not an issue. If required, it can be spent. However, we have to check with the other requirements, like we have to ascertain whether the TPA is open or not.'

Dr. Shah agreed, 'It will be helpful if you check those things beforehand. If the TPA is not open today, the medical insurance part will not be initiated. As a result, the billing department will not give the necessary clearance for the procedure.'

It was nearing ten. Sanjay promised to try their best. They did not have to strain themselves much as the medical insurance card itself contained the number of two individuals. It was the card given by Badshah's office which had all the relevant information regarding the TPA. It showed the names of Basant Kumar and Anand Prasad and their respective contact numbers.

The first person did not receive the call and the second expressed the inconvenience caused by the day. He wanted to harp on the festive atmosphere which had hampered the communication network necessary to resolve the case.

Left with no other alternative, they had to relinquish all hopes for Badshah's shunting for the day. Rintu and Sanjay had noticed that even the reception desk at Kokilaben was facing a shortage of staff. They were the ones who generally kept in touch with the TPA via phone calls or e-mails. In case of an operation or associated issues, they conveyed the estimate and got it approved or received the sanction for the same. If they were not present in sufficient numbers, invariably it would set off a crisis.

Rintu went to Dr Shah to inform him about the fiasco and to request the doctor to make preparations for the next day. Sanjay walked towards CCU 3. In the morning, they could not meet Badshah because of the consultation to be done with Dr. Shah. Sanjay felt a heart-rending urge to be with his son at that moment. Seeing his father, Badshah asked at once, 'Baba, where were you all this while?'

Sanjay softly replied, 'I came in the morning. You were sleeping at that time. How are you now, my son?'

With a frail voice, Badshah said, 'The headache has decreased a little. Baba, will my shunting happen today?'

'The headache has decreased a little. Baba, will my shunting happen today?'

Sanjay was at a loss for words. Should he speak the truth? Or should he explain it in an equivocating manner! Since their childhood, he had always encouraged his children to say what was true. Badshah loathed lying. But how could he reply to his ill son, who avidly sought emancipation from his crushing headache, and had asked his father a straightforward question, 'Baba, will my shunting happen today?'

Sanjay faced a serious quandary. The bitter truth might break his morale completely. Rather, for his well-being and to give him the necessary psychological support, Sanjay decided to compromise with his teachings. He paused a little and then said tactfully, 'It is scheduled to happen today. But, today being the first of January, all the required arrangements are proceeding at a snail's pace. Don't worry my boy. It will surely happen at the end of it all.'

Badshah remained silent. He fixed his gaze upon his father's face, as if, trying to scan the truth that lay hidden in it. In an attempt to avert his attention from the topic, Sanjay touched his son's head and tenderly brushed his fingers through Badshah's hair. Badshah closed his eyes, trying to savour the affection.

However, that pristine moment did not last for long. According to the rules, Sanjay had to come out of the CCU. It was almost twelve. Rintu was waiting outside. He got in after Sanjay emerged from the room. Sanjay told him that he would be at the canteen and instructed his brother to come there after meeting Badshah.

No sooner did he see Rintu than Badshah said, 'Happy New Year, Chotka!'

Trying hard to conceal his amazement, Rintu replied, 'Happy New Year, Badshah!' It was beyond his imagination that Badshah, rising above his misery, would wish him so spiritedly from the hospital bed. His face bore the imprint of intense pain. Yet his indefatigable nephew greeted Rintu heartily.

Earlier, such exchange of greetings did not take place between the father and the son. Whatever might be the reason, he could not wish his father. But within the CCU, nurses, all were continually repeating a plethora of 'happy new year' greetings among themselves. The exchange of wishes also included the patients, who were comparatively in a better condition. Badshah perhaps had observed the sudden burst of bonhomie. It might be possible that some of the doctors or nurses had also exchanged greetings with him. Rintu rightly surmised that all that had boosted the drooping spirit and got Badshah charged up enough to wish his uncle too.

Rintu was worried about the delay in shunting. Another day's loss meant a further increase in Badshah's agony. For the last twelve days he had been enduring the seasawing headache. Whenever it provided him some respite, he could chat with them and feel at ease. At other times, the headache intensified by leaps and bounds and Badshah fell silent. Sparingly, he blurted out exclamations of aahs and oohs, writhing in unbearable pain.

Rintu asked Badshah, 'Where are you feeling the pain now?'

Badshah took his uncle's right hand in his left and placed it on the left side of his head, 'Chotka, the trouble lies here.'

Rintu pressed his right hand against Badshah's head. It seemed that his nephew felt a bit relieved.

Towards the evening, Badshah asked Sanjay, 'Why didn't the shunting happen today?'

Sanjay was feeling shattered from inside. He did not want to face his son. Nevertheless, he trudged up to him. His innocuous query deeply distressed Sanjay. He gazed into the eyes of his son and slowly confessed, 'We tried hard, my dear, but all in vain.' Then, with both hands, he held the left hand of Badshah firmly. No words were spoken. By merely touching him with his hands, a father was trying to convey his failure, and his helplessness to his son. Not only that, it also seemed to be an ardent effort by the father, seeking desperately to transfer the poison which engulfed his son's body, into his own.

Badshah could sense the thoughts conveyed by his father's touch. He perfectly understood Sanjay's wretchedness. In better times, not incapacitated by drips and injections, he would have placed his right hand over Sanjay's hands. So, he resorted to his eyes to ring home the message. Widening his gaze, he looked at Sanjay. It was impossible to contain all that was expressed through those tale-telling eyes within a line or two. Perhaps the lines would never end. One seemed to imbibe the trust showered by a son to provide solace to his crestfallen father, 'Baba, you are giving it your all. What if things did not work out today? There is always tomorrow. I will somehow endure the pain for one more day.' Another was in the form of an assurance, 'Baba, don't worry. I am all right. Everything will be fine.'

Furthermore, there was perhaps an unstated line like, 'Baba, I am fine. How are you?'

Sanjay was forced to tear himself away from Badshah as the visiting time drew to a close. Showering lots of love on his son, he came out of the CCU.

It was decided that Sanjay and Mili would once again spend the night at Kokilaben while Rintu would return home.

Both of them remained restless and wide awake throughout the night. The following morning, Sanjay's request to meet Badshah was turned down by security. After a period of earnest pleading, he agreed to go inside and after some time brought the gloomy tidings from the sister. Badshah was in terrible agony for the entire night and kept calling his mother for solace. Towards the morning, he had fallen asleep.

A weary Sanjay felt even the worst of suffering was not without a limit. Beyond that, both the body and the mind get accustomed to misery. When that happens, suffering loses its sting. Or else, extreme fatigue sets in and takes control of the body as well as the mind. Was Badshah too going that way?

Sometime after, he took Mili to the canteen and ordered two cups of tea. Sanjay had made up his mind. The shunting should not be deferred any further. It had to happen on that day, as quickly as possible.

17

SHUNTING

...

The shunting eventually took place towards the evening. Rintu arrived early at the hospital to get conversant with the proceedings at the TPA counter. A suave young man of around twenty-five or six years, present at the counter, readily responded to his inquiry inquiry. Sanjay had already secured the estimate for shunting from the CCU. Along with that, he submitted Badshah's medical insurance card. The young man contacted the TPA in Bangalore and mailed the necessary details. A phone call was also made and Basanta Kumar assured them that he would get in touch with the insurance company and convey the development within an hour and a half. Sanjay utilized the interim period for a brief meeting with Dr Rajan Shah. He informed the doctor about the latest status. Dr Shah said, 'I will start the operation as soon as I receive the clearance from the billing department. Rest assured, there will be no delay in this regard on my part'.

Sanjay thanked him in advance and returned to that spacious waiting hall. He found Rintu there.

After one and a half hours, Sanjay phoned Basanta Kumar again. On the third attempt the call was received. Basanta Kumar said, 'Yes, I discussed with New India Assurance. According to them, the matter will take some time.'

Sanjay was deeply upset by the news. Sensing his distress, Mili, who was watching the proceedings from a sofa a little distance away, came beside Sanjay.

She enquired, 'What's wrong?'

Sanjay replied, 'Our country is in a pathetic condition. Nobody understands the meaning of a medical emergency. They said it would take an hour and now more than two hours have gone by just like that.'

Mili too felt perturbed. Her thoughts raced back to Badshah writhing in agony. She felt like going to her son. It was nearing midday. So, it was almost the time for the visiting hours to begin.

'Wait for a few more minutes,' Sanjay suggested, 'Then you might have some concrete information to cheer him up.'

Mili understood and said, 'Well, let us wait a bit more. Perhaps the formalities will be completed by then.'

Around half past twelve, news reached them from the TPA counter that the sanction had arrived. Rintu was provided with a printout by that affable young man.

'What's this! Only one lakh has been sanctioned whereas the estimate was for well above two lakhs!'

Rintu gave the printout to Sanjay, who was shocked! The estimate was attached with the mail and the same was also conveyed over the phone. Still it came down to one lakh which was barely half the sum required! Money was there in his account and he did have the debit card with him. He could have paid the remaining sum by swiping the card. But the question was, why was Badshah denied the entire sum? The insurance coverage was of a formidable sum of thirteen lakhs! Then why were they refusing to grant the entire amount at this early stage?

Upon enquiry ,they came to know that the insurance company, at first, provided a lump sum. In their parlance, this was akin to opening an account in the patient's name. That sum. in this case, was one lakh.

Acting on Rintu's suggestion, Sanjay rang up Amit Sachdeva. As always, Amit answered the call promptly and assured Sanjay he would quickly ring back with the details. He also asked about Badshah's condition and requested Sanjay to keep him updated as often as possible.

Within forty minutes Amit called back with the news that he had contacted the TPA and they in turn had a discussion with the insurance company. The remaining sum would be sanctioned in a short while. Sanjay glanced at his watch; it was almost two o' clock, the usual lunch time. It would take some more time for the intimation to arrive. He said to Mili and Rintu, 'Let us eat something.'

Rintu said, 'I had a heavy breakfast. So count me out; both of you go ahead.'

Quickly completing the eating formality, Sanjay rang up Basanta Kumar who informed him that the full amount had now been sanctioned. They had mailed the intimation to Kokilaben Hospital. Sanjay and Mili rushed to the billing department. After some anxious minutes, they met the young in charge and begged him to check the mail. At once he obliged. The mail stated that two lakh and fifteen thousand had been sanctioned for the operation.

Sanjay was thrilled to hear the information. He further requested the young man, 'Bhai, please send the news as fast as possible to the billing department.' Overwhelmed with mixed emotions, he addressed the in-charge as a brother, though he was almost of the same age as Badshah. But Sanjay was too preoccupied to rectify his mistake.

The young man looked at Sanjay and said, 'Uncle, I am forwarding it immediately.'

His comment felt like a soothing ice-rub on Sanjay's inflamed being. It seemed that someone had lit up a torch to show the way that had hitherto been utterly shrouded by darkness. There was no more impediment for the shunting to happen. His son would finally get the much-needed relief from the excruciating pain.

Rintu appeared before Sanjay could give him a call. Rintu went to the billing department and confirmed that they had indeed received the relevant e-mail. However, the department had some queries of their own for which they rang up CCU-3. After that discussion, Sanjay was asked to bring a form from the CCU on which the consent of the patient's nearest relative had to be taken.

Sanjay and Rintu scampered toward CCU-3. The sister in charge took considerable time to document a variety of information like the doctor's name, the name of his assistants, the history of the patient, etc. By the time they returned to the billing department, over an hour had passed and the watch showed five o' clock.

As soon as the clearance was given, Sanjay wasted no time in making a call to Dr Shah. The doctor was busy meeting patients in the outdoor section. He informed Sanjay of his plan to reach the CCU by six. Accordingly, everything should be kept ready and the operation would surely happen that evening.

In great relief, Sanjay sensed that the operation would commence pretty soon. He desperately wanted to give the news to the much-distressed Badshah. Who knows in what shape he is in? No matter what, Badshah needed to be informed that the shunting was to happen that day itself. Sanjay ran at top speed through the crowded waiting hall towards the lift. It seemed all around him everyone was conspiring to slow him down, without caring an iota about his worry! Somehow, Sanjay managed to reach the lift which appeared swarming with passengers. He had to let go of a trip but found space within the adjacent one that came down a few seconds later. He darted across the second floor and went racing into the CCU without paying any heed to the gatekeeper. The sister and ward boys were startled by his sudden, whirlwind entry. Sanjay, indifferent to their amazement, came to a stop only after he reached his son. Badshah's left hand was gingerly pressed against his head. A panting Sanjay blurted, 'Son, the shunting will happen this evening. Wait for a few minutes more for the doctor to arrive.

'This evening! Thank God.' Badshah's eyes lit up wonderfully. A splash of huge relief washed over his face.

All that Sanjay wanted was to see this sign of relief on his son's face. That was the reason for his desperate dash to convey the message of shunting to Badshah.

However, Sanjay was taken aback by the two words uttered by Badshah: 'Thank God'. Badshah does not believe in God. Sanjay, since the age of twenty-three, has been a confirmed atheist. At that time, he had read the book *Why I am an Atheist* by Bhagat Singh. Badshah was nurtured in the same way since his childhood. In a message of condolence, he wrote after the demise of his maternal grandmother, Badshah blatantly declared his atheism. Though he had heartfelt reverence towards his Dida's religiosity, Badshah suffered no qualms in laying bare his principles.

That same Badshah was voicing 'Thank God' at the most crucial juncture of his brief life! It was a development that amazed his father immensely. Was it a habitual expression that men do use now and then? Anything out of the ordinary gets a general 'Oh God' response. It was a commonplace utterance which according to Sanjay did not stem from any conviction. Rather it was a serious example of how one gets unconsciously influenced by something he listens to or is made to listen over a long period. Gradually this influence makes deep inroads and gets transformed into a notion. This notion relies more on habit than on conviction; this is known as habit force.

The thought kept pricking Sanjay. Was it the same with Badshah? It was not there at the beginning. Perhaps he had acquired the habit force later. Or it might be the case of Badshah's principles taking a U-turn! However, it did not seem like that to Sanjay.

Sanjay took Badshah's left hand within his palms and stood still for some time. Suddenly a sister appeared and said to Sanjay, 'The patient has to be taken to the O.T.'

Before taking leave, Sanjay tried his utmost to cheer up his son, 'Don't worry my boy. It is just a small operation. After this, everything will be fine again.'

Badshah acknowledged his father with a nod. As Sanjay advanced towards the waiting hall, a flicker of hope began to glow within him—after this, Badshah might get well soon!

After an hour and a half, Badshah was brought out of the O.T. into the CCU. The oxygen mask was firmly in place over his nose. He was still unconscious. Sanjay, Mili, and Rintu took turns to visit Badshah who seemed to be in deep sleep.

After some time, a junior doctor who had attended the operation informed them: 'Shunting successful.'

Sanjay asked, 'Have you inserted the programmable device inside Avik's brain?'

The doctor said, 'Yes, yes. Surely. As we had planned.'

Sanjay breathed a sigh of relief, 'Oh! After a prolonged period of agony will Badshah be able to sleep peacefully tonight.'

The sister added, 'None of you need to stay back tonight.'

Sanjay, Mili, and Rintu returned to Rintu's apartment. After several worry-riddled days, everyone would be able to get some meaningful rest.

The following morning, they came to the hospital around nine o'clock. Seeing Sanjay beaming at Badshah said, 'Baba, I am fine. Baba must say that the treatment at this hospital is excellent.'

Badshah's countenance radiated a sense of comfort. Sanjay caressed his son's head and agreed, 'Yes, Baba, this is obviously an excellent hospital.'

Sanjay noticed a tube-like structure at the back of Badshah's head. Sanjay came out and Mili went in next. Badshah was visibly elated to see his mother. With his left hand, he gripped the right hand of Mili and said, 'Did you return home last night?'

'Yes dear.' Mili replied as she held her son's left hand with both of her own.

'Did you sleep properly last night?'

'Probably yes. Can't remember exactly.'

Mili understood that it took a long time for consciousness to reappear completely. The heavy doses of medicines also played their part. It was quite natural that Badshah had little remembrance of the previous night.

Dr Shah arrived shortly and checked Badshah. After discussing with the sister, he appeared to look for Sanjay or Rintu.

Mili said, 'They are waiting outside. Let me send them inside.'

Mili left the CCU and immediately both the brothers came in.

Dr Shah said, 'The shunting procedure has been successful. The patient has got the necessary relief. I have collected the sample from inside the brain and sent it for biopsy. In my opinion, it is malignant, still we await the confirmation.'

Rintu asked, 'What is to be done if the biopsy report is positive?'

'Well, only an oncologist can give you the relevant advice. My part has been completed. Notwithstanding the outcome of the report, I will make arrangements to shift Avik tomorrow morning to a cabin. For today, I want to keep him under observation. The report will take at least two to three days to get ready.'

Rintu and Sanjay readily consented.

After meeting Badshah again, they came out of the CCU.

18

CABIN 12

•••

The following day, Badshah was shifted to a cabin. It was cabin number 12 on the twelfth floor. The numerical semblance made remembrance easier. Otherwise, it was extremely difficult to keep track of floors, cabins, CCU and OPD within the enormous hospital. Each cabin held two beds. One was near the door while the other was on the farthest end beside the window. Badshah got the one close to the door.

For the next three days, Badshah remained at ease, scarcely feeling pain or any related discomfiture. Some of his friends, mostly batchmates from the ISBM, turned up. Some were based in Mumbai whereas the others were working in the city. Badshah was overjoyed meeting them.

His left hand was busy greeting them. He heartily chatted and laughed with them.

However, his eyes yearned for some more endearing faces. Badshah wanted to meet his friends from Jamshedpur who worked in Bangalore and Monica, even though he did not express it verbally. His slightly better condition reminded Badshah of the days in Columbia-Asia. His cabin was always full of visitors who never failed to lift his spirits. His colleagues, football-mates, and friends from ISBM and Bangalore arrived in numbers to meet Badshah at the hospital. As always, their presence galvanized him and he endeavoured to retrieve his speaking abilities from the very next day of the surgery. Not only his friends, but Badshah also loved to embrace and greet all and sundry and in turn received their unbridled affection.

Here at Kokilaben, Badshah longed for those familiar faces. His eyes yearned to meet Rohan and Monica. From Delhi, Ruhi and Rajveer reached a day before Badshah was shifted to the cabin. He was very pleased to meet them. Badshah addressed Rajveer as 'Jiju'. Earlier, when his radiation-chemotherapy was on course at TMH, Rajveer doubled up as the physiotherapy guide for Badshah. Intent on regaining his former self, Badshah tried his best to complete the chores as instructed by his Jiju.

Badshah craved for such endearing sessions again, though he doubted whether his predicament would permit such practice. Still, feeling a little better, his mind continued to harp on such fond desires.

Sanjay and Mili discussed with Rintu and Badshah's uncle promptly suggested

Monica should be asked to come as soon as possible.

Sanjay rang up Monica on the 5th of January. She assured them that after arranging leave from her office, she would try to join them very quickly.

On the 7th of January, Monica arrived in Mumbai, making the journey by bus from Bangalore to Andheri. She carried a small bag on her shoulder containing a few essential things.

Sanjay tried to fight back his tears on seeing the resolute Monica. She was the girl Badshah was in love with. They shared the same city and workplace. In Bangalore, at the One's House located at Hormou, they even lived on different floors of the same building. If everything went well in Badshah's life, by now his marriage with Monica was a certainty. At Bappa's wedding, Sanjay almost made the announcement: 'Next year get prepared for Badshah's marriage ceremony. All of you must come to Jamshedpur.'

Everyone heartily agreed. Alas, how the times have changed. Badshah had to be rushed to Mumbai's Kokilaben Hospital; Monica had to depart from Bangalore to see Badshah. All these scenes were floating in front of Sanjay's eyes.

The presence of Monica thereby unsettled Sanjay.

'Kaku, please don't cry. Everything will be okay.'

Monica's comforting words helped Sanjay to regain his composure. Rintu took her to Badshah's cabin.

Badshah's joy knew no bounds when he saw Monica. He could scarcely believe that his fondest desire would turn into reality in this manner.

'Moni, it's you!'

'Yes, of course. You are in the hospital, how can I remain without seeing you?'

A gentle smile blossomed on Badshah's face and his eyelids quivered a bit. In a tender voice, he asked, 'How are you?'

'All right...Your Moni is all right.'

Monica, whom Badshah affectionately addressed as Moni, tried to make him feel comfortable.

Deep within her, an upheaval was wreaking havoc. Badshah had arrived in her otherwise gloomy life like a blessing. It was to be with Badshah that Monica came to Bangalore. She left her job and joined Badshah's company so that they could stay in proximity. It was a wonderful passage of time. They wandered here and there in the company of the friends from ISBM. Badshah loved to travel. He said, 'We learn a lot of things about new places from books. But to know the pulse and temperament of a place and its dwellers there is no better way than visiting that place. You have to freely mix with the people there and exchange ideas to know them in an all-encompassing manner, notwithstanding their virtues-vices, mindset, culture, habits, and inclinations. Mere reading cannot help you to tick all these boxes. That is why tourism has emerged as such an important sector.'

Monica readily seconded Badshah's views on traveling. Thus, they were always upbeat about visiting new places.

That once-vibrant Badshah was fighting for survival at the Kokilaben Hospital in Mumbai. Facing each other inside a cabin on the twelfth floor, words refused to tumble out of their turbulent minds. Talking was quite a strain for Badshah. Thousands of questions swirled inside Monica. It was not possible to share them with Badshah. His friends had already enlightened her a lot about the prognosis of grade 4 brain cancer.

Monica harboured high hopes for the radiation-chemotherapy treatment at TMH. She ardently believed that with the excellent medical support available there, there would surely be a positive development. Moreover, Badshah was a young, athletic individual trying desperately to recuperate. Monica felt all these would ensure the much-desired recovery.

Then why was there so much discussion about prognosis? Ritam, Rohan and others were repeatedly talking about the prognosis of this dreaded disease. Prognosis, to put it in a simple way, is pre-determination. In this case, perusing through the survival rate and relevant data, one can get a fair idea about the prognosis. She understood that their friends had made a considerable online study on the topic and were accordingly apprehensive. However, Monica's mind refused to agree. It revolted vehemently against accepting any unnerving thought.

This led to an unwelcome debate one day. Ritam-Rohan felt that Avik had very little chance of survival. As of now, medical science has no conclusive answer to this disease. He might survive a year or two. They had scanned the internet in search of any miraculous solution and instead met the brutal truth. Monica, though, refused to take it as an answer. She steadfastly held to her opinion that information available on the internet is not always accurate. Data, fed by humans, are logically prone to errors. Badshah had received the best treatment at TMH which enabled him to return to Jamshedpur. He was fine for a few months there. That gave her courage. Furthermore, Monica had unflinching faith in God, who, she felt would never allow her prayers to go in vain.

Yet, her heart started to beat faster as the news of Badshah's recent ailments reached her. The incessant headache and recurrent vomiting reminded her of what Ritam-Rohan said.

Recurrence is the worst thing to happen in Glioblastoma.

Had the same happened to Badshah? In Bangalore, such worries gave Monica little respite. Then came the news of Badshah being taken to Mumbai again, followed by the phone call. It was the 5th of December. Sanjay, whom she called Kaku, seemed a person undaunted by stiff challenges. During that formidable surgery of Badshah, Kaku's unruffled composure gave strength to all. The same Kaku sounded deeply distressed that day.

Monica immediately sensed the emergency and rushed to Mumbai. She did not pay any heed to her office's reluctance to grant her a long leave. She noticed the moist eyes of Sanjay the moment Monica stepped inside Kokilaben. She tried her utmost to console him though Monica could hardly manage to disguise her own tears. But she had to. She had to enter Badshah's cabin with a smile. Sitting beside the reclining Badshah, Monica remembered the message he had sent her a few months ago. It was: 'Moni, it is a litmus test for us. Don't give up, neither will I, love you the most.'

Monica never gave up. She steadfastly tied herself to the hope that Badshah would get well. She defied the information on the internet, she defied everyone and everything.

Badshah was also putting up a brave fight. Amidst all the agony, he did not give up his will to survive. Enduring chemo of such high doses, Badshah kept on smiling and conversing with others. He diligently co-operated in every step of the treatment. He admirably endured a massive surgery, thirty-three rounds of radiation, forty-five rounds of chemo, and even an MRI four times. Never for a moment did Badshah let go of his courage. Never did he express fear. His right hand and leg had lost their mobility and yet a resolute Badshah bore the challenges of physiotherapy, digging deep into the reserves of his patience.

For the umpteenth time, Monica opened the message box on his mobile to read that message. She glanced at Badshah's face. Was he fatigued? Was he feeling devastated from within? It appeared that Badshah had lost considerable ground in this battle. Monica was in excruciating pain watching the silent figure whose closed eyes unnerved her absolutely. She let out a wail though no words came out, 'Avik, please remember, this is our litmus test. We cannot accept defeat. We cannot give up. We have to overcome this ordeal.'

There was a knock on the cabin door. A sister entered with some medicines. The young sister smiled at Monica who returned the same gesture. Badshah had opened his eyes at the sound of the knocking. The sister started to inject the medicines into the drip tube fastened on his left hand.

Outside the cabin, darkness started to descend slowly. The visiting hours had begun. The air gradually got heavy with the sound of a plethora of footsteps.

19

CCU

•••

Badshah almost stopped eating from the next day. Everyone tried to persuade him, but in vain. Moreover, it seemed unwise to press on with the request after the vigorous bouts of vomiting Badshah suffered one day when he tried to comply with Sanjay's pleadings. After the vomiting subsided, he looked at Sanjay and said, 'See what happens whenever I make an effort to eat!'

Sanjay had no answer. An aged lady doctor was regularly supervising Badshah after he was shifted to the cabin. She repeatedly urged, 'Avik, you have become very weak. You have to increase your food intake.'

Her name was Jyoti Oak. She was from Kashmir and her graceful appearance affirmed that she was quite a stunner in her youth. Her assuring manner of talking gave the impression that Badshah was merely down with typhoid and not cancer. So, by eating properly, he would get well soon. Badshah and even Sanjay were somewhat influenced by her positivity.

Dr Oak was a general physician and not an oncologist. Thus, she was seeing things from her perspective. However, Badshah desperately needed an oncologist for consultation at Kokilaben. Their search resulted in the meeting with Dr Seema Limaye. When she checked Badshah for the first time, he remained taciturn. She herself felt quite crestfallen. Coming out of the cabin, Dr Limaye informed Sanjay and Mili, 'Your son has started to withdraw. You must be aware of the prognosis of this disease. So you don't have much time left for the inevitable to happen. Time gets further reduced once the patient begins the withdraw. Please don't mind, this is, as I perceive, the situation with your son.'

Tears obscured everything around Sanjay and Mili. Dr Limaye saw that and felt extremely disconcerted. She tried her best to console them, 'You have done everything possible for his treatment. Batting all odds, you came from Jamshedpur to Mumbai to give him the appropriate treatment. Very few can actually do so much. This is indeed a fatal disease that spares no one. Please prepare your mind for the inevitable.'

Dr Limaye rested her hand, like a dear relative, on Mili's shoulder. Mili tried to accept the doctor's advice. For the last ten months, they had waged a formidable war against this terrible foe. They had refused to yield even after knowing the possible consequences of their son's ailment. There was a belief that the highly esteemed treatment at TMH would surely work wonders. Badshah himself was upbeat about his recovery and never allowed any negativity to dampen his spirit.

But, since their arrival in Mumbai, things had started to change from bad to worse. After the disappointment at Nanawati, they depended wholeheartedly on TMH. Slowly, the faith eroded away. Not only did they fail to arrange the shunting due to the paucity of programmable devices but they also failed to provide any assurance regarding saving Badshah's life. After the shunting, they had gone through the biopsy report provided by Kokilaben, but it said nothing new. As per the custom at TMH, every month a meeting of doctors is held to discuss selective cases and decisions are taken about new measures. Last month, Badshah's case was discussed in that meeting. The following day, Sanjay, Rintu, Ruhi and Rajveer went to the hospital to learn about the outcome of the meeting. They had pinned their hopes on a positive development but were utterly shattered to hear the same information, 'Badshah has no chance of survival.'

Now Dr Limaye also echoed that piercing statement, 'Please prepare your mind for the inevitable.'

After the doctor left, Sanjay and Mili dumped themselves on a sofa outside the cabin. A devastating tempest was tearing everything apart inside them. Their eyes were shut but tears breached them ceaselessly. They could hear the marauding footsteps of an approaching earthquake. It was going to be an all-annihilating earthquake.

Shortly afterward, Monica came to them and said, 'I would like to stay in Avik's cabin tonight.'

Yesterday Mili had stayed back as Monica was advised to rest for she had endured a long bus journey from Bangalore.

Sanjay said, 'All right. Tonight, you stay here.'

Once the visiting hour was over, they returned to Rintu's flat. The next day, Sanjay woke up late. The continuous stress of the last few days had to be shaken off through extended rest. Mili was already up and Sanjay's sleep was slowly effaced by her conversation with Monica. Three words nailed his ears, Seizure, CCU, and Ventilation.

Monica gradually informed Sanjay that around two a.m., Badshah suffered a seizure. His entire body became stiff and the eyes appeared to jump out from their sockets. Terrified, Monica immediately informed the nurse on duty outside the cabin. On seeing his critical condition, the nurse administered an injection. The doctor rushed in, checked his condition, and instructed him to shift Badshah to the CCU. Around five in the morning, Badshah was placed in CCU 10, bed number 47. Monica was not allowed to stay back at the CCU. She waited for some time at the lounge and returned home at seven.

Sanjay, Mili and Rintu reached the hospital in an auto at eleven o'clock. CCU 10 was on the 10th floor. However, the lift was not available as the visiting hour was at twelve and only then would the lift start to operate. Eventually, when they arrived at the tenth floor, they met a fairly squarish area. CCU 10 was on the left of the lift.

The visitors were given small brass discs that served as the gate pass. It also contained the bed numbers. Badshah's bed number was 47.

47 was a number that Sanjay, like any other Indian, held very close to his heart. In 1947, India got her independence from the British after a monumental struggle laced with sacrifice. However, the magic of the number failed to rejuvenate Sanjay's melancholic mind as he entered the CCU.

The pitiable sight that met him inside the CCU soured his mind further. On both sides, critical patients, mostly on ventilation, were fighting for their lives. Few patients were partly conscious. Their countenance was a grim picture of intense agony.

Badshah's bed was quite a distance away from the door. A wide space was surrounded by a side screen to make room for a pair of beds on both sides. Badshah's bed was beside the wall. A huge glass was there on the wall instead of a window. Glancing through it one could see a big ground. A huge building, perhaps that of a school, stood a little distance away from the ground.

Badshah was almost unconscious. A rubber pipe was placed on one corner of his mouth to keep the oxygen flow going. Another pipe, for nasal feeding, was placed inside his nostril. Drip was being administered on his right hand. It was a distressing sight for once Badshah regained his senses, he would feel acutely uncomfortable. Sanjay took his left hand and held it silently for some time. Then he tenderly kissed Badshah's forehead and came out.

Rintu and Mili, in turn, went in to meet Badshah and came out with tears in their eyes. It was almost one in the afternoon. Sanjay rang up Ruhi and informed her to come along with Rajveer in the evening. The visiting hour for the afternoon session was almost over. So, they too, were on their way back.

In the evening, after the visiting hour was over, Monica rushed towards the Siddhi Vinayak Mandir. The shrine was not only a must-visit for the Mumbai dwellers but also for devotees across the world. They believed that their heartfelt prayers would not go unanswered here! Monica too had heard of the place. She could not even think of a life without Badshah. Their sublime love for each other was an everlasting truth. A plethora of dreams did they share between them.

Monica refused to give up, to accept the writing on the wall. Badshah was still fighting and so should she. Medical science might fail to cure him, and the doctors might resign Badshah's case to fate but still, there was her unwavering faith in divine providence. God would never desert her side or else what was the Almighty there for?

Everyday Monica said her prayers to the idol of Ganesh, which was placed on the left of the entrance to Kokilaben.

Monica repeated the prayers whenever she found herself beside Badshah's bed.

Ruhi loved her brother dearly and called him 'bhai'. Badshah too, was very fond of his didi. Sometimes, he called her 'pidi'. In his mobile, Ruhi's number was saved as 'didi my pide'.

Ruhi almost lost her mental stability in this crisis. She could scarcely cope with the thought of losing her dear brother. Otherwise an atheist like Badshah, started to practice 'chanting'. Ruhi picked the information from someone that this form of prayer, as advocated by the Buddhists, could heal even those whose days were numbered.

Ruhi begins to 'chant' whenever and wherever possible and for a number of times a day.

Meanwhile, Badshah remained on ventilation. He was being fed through the pipe. Medicines were administered through injection. He continued in a semi-conscious state for a week and a half. Then one day, making everyone euphoric, Badshah came out of the ventilation. It seemed that the much-sought-after miracle had happened at last.

Within a couple of days of Badshah going into ventilation, Ruhi and Rajveer undertook a venture. To combat the enormous cost of treatment at the CCU in Kokilaben, they made a general appeal through Facebook providing the details of Badshah's treatment. Their aim was to form a fund. The response was overwhelming indeed. People donated generously. Ruhi's own post also received similar acknowledgment. The individuals who sent money also enthusiastically followed the updates made by Ruhi regarding Badshah.

When Badshah came out of the ventilation and Ruhi shared the joyous news, her post was inundated with more than six hundred 'likes'.

However, within a few hours, Badshah was put on the ventilator again. In the short interim, they all went to meet him. Badshah saw Mili and merely asked, 'Maa, when will I go home?'

His voice was drenched in tears. Mili, suppressing an abyss of grief, could only answer, 'See, you are gradually getting well. Wait for a few days more and we will take you home.'

Badshah fell silent.

Two weeks passed by. Sanjay, Mili, Rintu, Ruhi, and Rajveer kept visiting the unconscious Badshah in the morning and evening. Monica had to return to Bangalore as her office was unwilling to extend the leave. Her mind however remained rooted at Kokilaben.

The doctors, however hopeless the patient's condition might be, never fail to continue with their process of treatment. It was the same in Badshah's case. Every day one or the other pathological examinations followed. Blood tests, ECG, and CT scans went on every now and then. The findings sometimes showed a fall in sodium level or a dip in platelet count. Sometimes the heartbeat had to be regularized. Present-day medical science relies on supervising the functioning of the organs and putting them back to order, whenever necessary. During the last days of Badshah's life, what Sanjay saw seemed to him more of a damage-control exercise than an effective treatment. Was not this a process that served only to delay the patient's demise? Sanjay sensed that the question held little meaning at present. One day, medical science will unravel the reason or the cause behind such fatal diseases. Yes, the war has to be fought not against the consequences but the cause itself.

The present-day world, blindfolded by the maddening pursuit of power was indifferent about such requirements. Decisions in matters of importance like food, clothing, shelter, health, and education are still being taken sidestepping the requirements of the masses. It is quite baffling to think about the objectives of such pompous plans and who they really serve.

After seeing Badshah, Sanjay sat on the sofa in the waiting hall and reflected on these issues. He saw so many helpless people around him. They had come from near and far, waiting with the hope of taking their near and dear one's home one day, alive and fully cured. The huge expenditure is a constant challenge though they continue to wrestle with it by mortgaging all that they have. Sanjay could not help wondering, 'Why does treatment have to be so expensive? Why those concerned do not give the matter a proper thought?'

He himself knew how many go bankrupt while trying to meet the escalating cost of treatment of their loved ones.

Does anybody care to bother how medical treatment today, like other services, has become a 'saleable commodity'? Suddenly, he remembered what Badshah had said once. It was long before he fell sick. Possibly it was 2015 when Badshah took a leave and returned to Jamshedpur. The father-son duo was sharing their views on the national economy and the job market. It was then that Badshah had said, 'Baba, working in corporate sector means to keep on selling one product of the company, regardless of the product being a goods or service.'

After all this time, Sanjay experienced a fresh understanding of what his son had said that day.

20

VENTILATION

...

Three weeks went by but Badshah could not come out of ventilation. To prevent any infection from the mouthpiece, a small opening was made in his throat. A pipe was inserted through it, which would enable the direct passage of oxygen into his lungs, thereby helping Badshah to breathe. However, such a setting ensured that he would not be able to talk.

However, during the dire time, Badshah did regain consciousness a few times. Some of his friends and well-wishers visited him during that phase. Seeing the known faces around him, his joy and excitement was reflected on his face, though he was unable to express the same in words. He was especially inverogated to see his ISBM batchmate and dear friend Rupak. After trying extremely hard to find his voice, a dejected Badshah gestured his friend's attention towards his throat. Perhaps, he was desperate to say some final words as Badshah by then had become sure of his fast-approaching end.

One day, during the visiting hour, Sanjay found Badshah sitting on his bed. This was a common sight at CCU10 in Kokilaben. Critical patients and even those barely conscious were somehow helped into a seating position on a chair-like thing, on the bed itself.

Badshah was sitting on such a bed-chair and he was conscious too. Making an effort to boost up his flagging spirits, Sanjay said, 'Badshah, you have to come out of this. You have struggled a lot, my dear, just brace yourself for a little more, just a little. I know, you can and you will.'

Badshah shrugged his shoulder as much as he could as if to express, 'No.

It is beyond me to continue the fight anymore. No, I can't.'

That day, Mili, after much insistence, was allowed to enter with Sanjay. Perhaps the gateman softened a little, perceiving Badshah's age and precarious condition. Badshah noticed them coming. Thus, in response to his father's request, he did not lose a second to gather all the strength left in him to declare to his parents, 'I am leaving.'

Nothing was left for Mili and Sanjay to understand. As Mili tried to embrace Badshah, tears gushed forth. Sanjay failed to control himself and made his way out of the CCU.

Sanjay became certain that Badshah had understood that he would be passing away in no time. The saga of apprehension that began at Nanawati Hospital was drawing to its fatal end.

The incessantly agonizing question was: would Badshah survive? Yet Sanjay never gave up. Even when the doctors gave their verdict in unison, he still hoped for a miracle to happen. Medical science is full of such unbelievable tales of survival. Who knows, Badshah's case might become one such story too! Moreover, the patient's will to live plays a decisive role. From the very first day, Badshah had refused to yield. Very few can bear the trauma of brain MRI, with the head remaining inserted within a claustrophobic, dark tunnel for forty-forty-five minutes. A single minute seems like an age. Many otherwise brave and robust individuals suffer nervous breakdowns and keep on screaming for release before the scheduled time.

Badshah had endured the MRI four times. He remained calm and composed, defying his acute discomfort, and always inserted his head into the machine with a smile.

Similarly, most patients are unable to leave their bed after absorbing high doses of chemo. They almost become incapacitated. However, even after tolerating such severe doses of chemo, Badshah manifested a cheerful disposition towards his friends and neighbours who visited him. He did get out of his bed and joined them in conversation. He had the rare gift of effortlessly suppressing all grief within him.

The same young man, that day, flatly rebutted Sanjay's entreaty and instead conveyed signs about his ultimate farewell. Unable to speak, he shook his head in rejection, as if to say, 'I am not staying anymore.'

Sanjay received the unmistakable message that the tireless fighter Badshah, who had been putting up a stiff resistance against the invincible disease, had decided to hang up his boots once and for all.

This is how innumerable brave hearts ultimately succumb to this killer disease. Not only that, even the twenty-first century medical science that otherwise occupies a lofty position in the ever-developing world of science keeps on suffering ignoble losses at the merciless hands of this ruthless disease.

A father's monumental struggle, aspirations, and efforts paled into insignificance in front of it. The reality of medical limitations annihilated all that Sanjay could hope for. Even the minute possibility of saving his only son evaporated into thin air. It seemed like the dictum of destiny which Sanjay had neither the might nor the means to challenge!

Within three days Badshah was relegated into a coma. Dr Shah sent a message to Sanjay to meet him. Sanjay was well aware of the reason though he responded accordingly. At a distance from Badshah's bed, nearly half a dozen doctors were present around Sanjay, when he was briefed that the patient was in an extremely critical condition. Anything could happen at any moment. Sanjay had no doubt what the word 'anything' exactly meant. Without enquiring either about the treatment or the patient, Sanjay kept on listening. Earlier he had many discussions with Dr Shah regarding the patient's conditions as well as the details of the treatment. But that day, he kept silent. There was nothing more to say or to know. Badshah himself had given the ominous signal to him. Through the blurred corners of his eyes, Sanjay saw the shrunken face of Dr Shah. Melancholy was also writ large across the faces of the junior doctors. For who can accept such a fate of a twenty-eight-year-old vibrant young man? Did not the limitations of treatment pain them immensely? Were they not appalled by their helplessness to prevent such an irrevocable loss?

With a heavy heart, Sanjay left the CCU. Before that, he looked at Badshah but could not see his face entirely. From the little that Sanjay saw, it appeared that Badshah was sleeping peacefully.

Sanjay returned to Rintu's place. Mili, who saw him coming, understood everything and chose not to make any inquiry. After having a wash and changing his dress, Sanjay sat reclining on the bed. Mili came into the room and sat next to him quietly. After some time, she asked,

'Do you want to have tea?'

Sanjay shook his head. Suddenly Mili heard him singing:

A restless fish

knew well the stooping tree

by the river-side
played the fish
now and then
the tree bent and saw
knew, played, bent, and saw
isn't it all a tale from the past, isn't it
then tell me what is left for the present? What remains?
Men do know, men do know…

Mili was startled! This was unmistakably a song by Kabir Suman.

This was also the last song hummed by Badshah. He couldn't restrain himself from singing even on the hospital bed. Being in that parlous situation, he could not stay away from songs. That day his discomfort gave Badshah a brief respite. Perhaps that enabled him to sing the entire song.

Sanjay looked at Mili after the first four lines were completed. At once they sensed the context of the song. Both of them were present when Badshah was singing that day.

Sanjay could remember that he was feeling a bit unwell the following day. Though he had wanted to, Mili and Rintu advised him against visiting the hospital. Sanjay was alone in the flat. Badshah asked Mili about his father's absence. Mili rang up Sanjay. Badshah took the phone and asked, 'Baba, how are you?'

That was the final time Badshah spoke to his father. The following night Badshah suffered a seizure and by the morning he was shifted to the CCU.

In the CCU, Badshah and Sanjay never got an opportunity to talk with each other again. Badshah was not in a position to speak, with a pipe inserted in his mouth followed by another pipe inserted through his neck. Once, for a few hours, Badshah could come out of the ventilation. That was the time he had asked his mother, 'When will I go home?'

Sanjay heard about it from Mili.

Reminiscences fleeted across Sanjay's mind like a film. The scenes kept on coming even when his eyes remained shut.

Perhaps, sitting beside him, Mili was lost in similar thoughts. It is quite possible that the mother's mind had gone backward to the days of Badshah's birth. He used to look around in wonder. When he grew up a little, Badshah used to storm around the house in a walker. Then came the day when, wearing a uniform, he took small steps towards his school. In the evenings, Badshah sat down to complete his homework and diligently got ready for school again. Mili could not remember a single incident of Badshah giving her a tough time. She never had to raise her voice about anything to Badshah. He had the unique capacity accepting to accept the simple truths of life. His little frame could easily absorb all the good things of life.

Once in the school magazine, one of his friends wrote about Badshah, 'Every good thing in a small package.'

Both Mili and Sanjay had read that piece of writing that superbly brought out the sterling qualities of Badshah.

Badshah keenly watched the football leagues across Europe on television. He possessed all the latest trivia related to the English Premier League, La Liga, and Bundesliga. He knew almost all the players. Badshah loved to study the history of the famous football clubs. This was how his love for Arsenal started to grow. Badshah was fascinated to know that in order to establish their rights to play football, the labourers and workers of that place formed the Arsenal Football Club. That made them different from Manchester United or Chelsea. Badshah scarcely missed an Arsenal match. He posted a lot about football and Arsenal on Facebook. He was such an avid fan of Arsenal that even at Columbia-Asia Hospital, Monica made arrangements to tie the Arsenal tag in his cabin. She knew that would cheer him up immensely.

Sanjay remembered that day in Bangalore when Dr Raghuraman came to visit Badshah after the surgery. It was then that he noticed the Arsenal tag and got informed about Badshah's devotion. He admitted himself a hearty laugh and added, 'Nowadays when everyone else seems busy with cricket at least there is one who has remained sincere in his love for football. This is simply great!'

Along with the others present, Badshah too broke into a laugh. He had no clue that his passion for football would receive such a rapturous acknowledgmentacknowledgment from the doctor.

Anecdotes and memories in bits and pieces continued to swell up within Mili and Sanjay. Though they were not the same always they were definitely tied by a common thread. They were snippets that manifested the pure simplicity, politeness, generosity, and magnanimity that blended together to make Badshah such a unique young man.

The same Badshah was bidding farewell to one and all. Mili could still hear him calling out 'Maatey'—Badshah's special term of endearment for his mother. That address had a magical attraction, it used to bring her son closer to her; the call made him her very own.

Though summoned for dinner, Sanjay and Mili had no appetite. Still, they sat at the table with Rintu. Sanjay had heard about alternative medicine. Badshah's friends were hopeful about its outcome. Meanwhile, Rajveer had gone to an Ayurvedic outlet at Juhu-Tara Road. Sanjay and Rintu went to another outlet at Andheri-East. They refrained from buying the medicine eventually, for they had no faith in them. Still, as the saying goes in Hindi: *Marta kya nahi karta?*

Sanjay revived the topic at dinner. Rintu said, 'Well, let us go there in the evening.'

Accordingly, Sanjay and Rintu bought the ayurvedic medicine from the Juhu-Tara Road outlet. The next challenge was to give the medicine to Badshah which would be a direct violation of the rules regarding medicines supplied from outside at Kokilaben. Everything was scanned at the main entrance. Fooling the security was out of the question.

Thus, they sought the help of the CEO and he in turn consulted Dr Shah to approve their request. The doctors in charge of CCU were given the necessary instructions. Everybody fully co-operated, setting aside all cynicism. The potion provided in ten bottles was blended together to prepare the required dose. The sisters present within the CCU also assisted in the preparation and ensured its appropriate supply through the nasal pipe.

For the next three days, Badshah was given the medicine in the morning and evening. However, the efforts went in vain as Badshah gradually sank into a deep coma. At last, on 13 February 2017, at around quarter to twelve in the morning, Rintu got a phone call from the hospital. By then Sanjay and Mili had already set out to reach there within the visiting hour. As they were waiting in the hall downstairs for the clock to strike twelve, Rintu rang up and said, 'Wait for me. I am coming.'

Rintu arrived at Kokilaben within twenty minutes. Then he said, 'I will be returning shortly from upstairs. Till then, sit here and wait for me.'

At once, Rintu rushed towards the lift that would take him to CCU 10.

Sanjay and Mili said nothing. They looked at each other in silence. It was all too clear. The moment Rintu called them up, they understood the reason—Badshah had passed away.

21

ARSENAL

...

Rintu, responding to the calling bell, opened the door. A courier service man stood outside with a big packet.

He said, 'Sir, there is a letter.'

Rintu checked his name and address on it. His surprise knew no bounds when he found that the sender's address was Arsene Wenger, Arsenal Football Club!

What was going on? What was sent to him by this legendary football club? Rintu unwrapped the packet slowly. There was a photo card which contained the pictures and autographs of all the current Arsenal footballers. It was absolutely star-studded, comprising names like Aaron Ramsay, Mesut Ozil, Alexis Sanchez,

Danny Welbeck, and Lucas Perez. There was a letter too. It was addressed to Badshah, and penned by the inimitable Arsene Wenger himself. The venerable manager of Arsenal had expressed deep concern about Badshah's ailment and also conveyed their best wishes for a speedy recovery. Rintu felt extremely surprised and touched by the incident.

The letter was written on 25 January. Badshah had been alive then. He passed away on 13 February 2017 and the letter reached Rintu on 18 February. Perhaps there was a delay in posting the letter or a problem with the delivery system itself which had caused the late arrival.

Whatever the reason, the letter itself was a puzzle. He was aware of the fact that Badshah was an ardent fan of Arsenal. His passion for the club became vehemently vivid during his struggle against the deadly disease. However, this letter in itself was no small matter.

Famous football clubs enjoy both national and global fan following. Their ardent admirers are spread far and wide across the globe. Still, such a gesture was almost unheard of that the club had taken the initiative of sending one of its critically ill supporters such an endearing letter, that too with autographed pictures of its players!

Later, Sanjay informed him that it was Prasun, a dear friend of Badshah, who had mailed to Arsenal about his illness. Prasun was well aware of Badshah's admiration for Arsenal. He also wrote extensively to the club about Badshah's posts on Facebook that showcased his love for

Arsenal and football. The letter was in response to that mail. Rintu could not help thinking that if Badshah had been alive, a letter from Arsenal wishing his speedy recovery could have sent him to cloud nine!

Ten months later, an emergency engagement brought Sanjay to Mumbai again. During an evening, walking aimlessly, he found himself near Char-Bungalow. Lost in thought, Sanjay failed to notice the sprawling presence of the Kokilaben Hospital on his right-hand side. Sanjay's preoccupied mind was abruptly pierced by an all-too-well-known call: Baba, how are you?

Yes, yes, it was unmistakably the voice of Badshah! Sanjay looked upwards, trying to follow the call. There it was, that huge glass window of the CCU. CCU 10 on the 10th floor! The large playground was still enjoying the company of some boys continuing with their game in the fast-fading light. There was Badshah, on that floor—for over a month—bed number-47. Sanjay felt it was from there that the call had reached him.

Sanjay had no belief in the soul, the existence of a divine soul, or possibility of re-incarnation. Then how did it happen question a baffled Sanjay asked himself. Since Badshah was diagnosed with Glioblastoma, the question has been gnawing away at Sanjay's mind. The answer eludes him. The answer eludes all. Once the disease makes you its prey, there is no respite, only 'no' and 'no' keep on piling.

But why it should be like this? Why should the world meekly bow down to this 'no'? Human beings are visiting the moon, sending spacecraft to other planets, and inventing superior means of destruction at will. Why do they keep on failing miserably in this respect? The will to find an answer and to find a solution to this overwhelming question is what gives Sanjay a cause to live for.

Badshah echoed the same inquiry. Sanjay could feel the presence of his son within him acutely. As if allowing his unconscious mind to take over, Sanjay screamed from within, 'No son, I am not feeling well. Not feeling well at all.'

Continuing his profound conversation with Badshah, Sanjay confessed, 'Remember son, you only said the other day that Baba, everything has become a product. The whole world as well as our own lives are all products. Yes, dear beta, Glioblastoma did not invade your brain only, today, this entire world has been afflicted with Glioblastoma.'

At heart, Sanjay perceived how Glioblastoma has contaminated the flow of life. Its overwhelmingly toxic presence has spread everywhere. Life force stands no chance against this omnipotent adversary. Sanjay looked upwards at that huge glass window on the tenth floor and muttered, 'Nobody is feeling well, my son, nobody is keeping well!'

Arsenal

ARSENAL FOOTBALL CLUB
HIGHBURY HOUSE
75 DRAYTON PARK
LONDON N5 1BU

TELEPHONE: +44 (0)20 7619 5003
FAX: +44 (0)20 7704 4001
www.arsenal.com

Avik Roy
C/O Mr Sumit Roy
33-34 Movie Towie
Yamuna Nagar
Lokhandwala
Andheri West
Mumbai Maharshtra 400053
India

25th January 2017

Dear Avik

I have been informed that you have not been very well recently. I am very sorry to hear this and on behalf of everyone at Arsenal Football club I send you best wishes.

I have also been told that you are an avid Arsenal supporter. We are extremely grateful for this. As a token of our appreciation please find enclosed a photo of the team which thy have signed fort you.

On behalf of the players, staff and management at Arsenal Football Club, once again I send you best wishes and thank you for your continued support; it is greatly appreciated.

Yours sincerely

Arsene Wenger
Manager of Arsenal Football Club

Thy Name Is Life

ACKNOWLEDGMENT

•••

Any story is truly an amalgamation of a lifetime of experiences, a million little moments that made an impact and contributed to it in some small way or another. This story is not an outcome of a father's bereavement; rather, it is a mixture of the eight-month-long battle fought by Avik and all those who were close to him. To mention all those who were a part of this journey would be an impossible task. However, there are a few who just have to be mentioned, as they played a big role in shaping this book, directly or indirectly.

To my wife, Shyamali, without whose incessant inspiration and cooperation, this book would not have seen the light of day.

To my brother, Sumit, who played an exigent role throughout the difficult journey. Since the deadly disease was detected until the very end, 'Chotka' was a sanctuary for Avik.

To Mrs. Sreejata Guha, who took it upon herself to translate this piece of my heart into English, to broaden the horizons of this book.

To Mr. Samrat Maitra, who assisted Mrs. Guha tirelessly in bringing the English edition of the book to life.

To Ms. Tania Dutta, who extended her helping hand with her incisive inputs.

Thy Name Is Life

SYNOPSIS

•••

Did he find his lIfe In the game of soccer? Or he used to explore life by mingling with the people around him? Probably both.

While watching soccer, been played in various parts of the world, he became a die hard fan of Arsenal Football Club of London, being impressed by their struggling history. On the other hand, giving up his dream of beingg a great footballer due to financial hardships, he acquireda job of a financial analyst in a US based company. He commenced his career there industriously and by virtue of his virtuosic performance, bagged a promotion within a short spell. He became very popular amongst his colleagues and beyond. He also led the office football team to victory in Bengaluru Office Soccer League.

It was in the end of April 2016 that Avik found his right hand and lower limb not functioning wella.ll . Getting no result from medicines, he had to undergo MRI followed by surgery and thus it was detected malignant cancer that too of a very rare kind, Glloblastoma. The family decided to get him treated at TMH Bombay, but trouble was still round the corner. 'The block' which was given for biopsy was not handed over to the family even on the day they were leaving for Mumbai. Thus began Avik's and his family's long battle with the deadly disease. After two long, painful months of undergoing radiation and chemotherapy, it seemed that Avik had finally won the battle and the family returned to their base. But little did they know that this joy was a short lived one. While Avik was trying his level best to get his former strength back, his nightmare' was just lurking inin the shadows and planning his' deadly onslaught. This brought him back to Mumbai His last hope was to undergo shunting which provided temporary repose.

But Avik could not win the deadly battle. Avik Roy died 42 days after his shunting, in the ICU, when the ccaa ncer which was made of him, finally stopped his heart, which was also made of him, creating a huge vacuum in the hearts of the people he had touched.

THE END

www.ingramcontent.com/pod-product-compliance
Lightning Source LLC
LaVergne TN
LVHW061540070526
838199LV00077B/6850